BITCH HUNT

BITCH HUNT

TAETRECE HARRISON

Harrison
Publishing, L.L.C.

Paperback: ISBN: 979-8-9864883-0-1

Hardcover: ISBN: 979-8-9864883-1-8

eBook: ISBN: 979-8-9864883-2-5

Audiobook: ISBN: 979-8-9864883-3-2

Second edition, August 20th, 2022

Published by Harrison Publishing, L.L.C.

www.taetreceharrison.com

The Women I Know

The women I know

Are strong and proud

They have walked through the mud of life and environment

Only to emerge, victorious

They have suffered the slings and arrows of adversity and wrong

Stumbling but not going down.

Loving, Living, Prospering

The women I know

The women I know

Continue to grow

They flourish from the bottom of the pit to the top of the mountain

The women I know

The women I know

Continue to persevere no matter what

The women I know

Continue to grow

The women I know

They stumble, they fall

The women I know stand in their truth

Stand up with convictions against those who want no growth

Some may fall and fight no more

But some may even crawl but they never forget the prize, the cause

They keep going ever moving upward, always, always

But most will do their best in the face of uncertainty and push back

Continuing to flourish, always

Continuing to grow

The Women I know

The Women I know

~Donnias Harrison

Acknowledgments

I want to say to my mother, Donnias M. Harrison, thank you for all the wisdom, love and support you have given me.

To my sister, Schalyece M. Harrison who always has my back no matter what. Also, I offer my sincere gratitude to my sister, Treschere T. Harrison and my brother, Aaron J. Harrison, Jr.

To my son, Randyn J. Johnson, I love you!

I am eternally grateful to my colleague and friend, Jacqueline Epstein, for giving me the idea to write this book.

I want to say thank you to my developmental editor, Jamie Iredell, for pushing me to do my absolute best writing.

To my cousin, Nonetta M. Pierre for always being available to help without hesitation. Also, my cousins, Dana M. Pierce and DeJean Pierce for being very supportive at every point of my writing this book.

My heartfelt thanks and constant encouragement to my friends but more like family, Kelly Brossett, Lydia Glapion, Nikki Krivjanick, Nelita Manego Ramey and Eleanor Salahuddin.

My warmest gratefulness to an impressive artist who captured the vision for my book cover, Varion Laurent.

Contents

The Women I Know .... *vii*

Acknowledgments .... *xi*

CHAPTER ONE 1

January 30, 2018 1

September 28, 2017 1

October 9, 2017 5

October 12, 2017 6

October 12, 1967 7

January, 2000 8

October - December 2017 9

December 13, 2017 12

January 4, 2018 14

January 30, 2018 16

CHAPTER TWO 29

October 14, 2017—Primary Election 40

November 18, 2017-Election Day 43

CHAPTER THREE 47

August 2014 47

1960s 48

1990s 49

2011 51

2012 53

August 4, 2014 54

June 13, 2017 56

June 15, 2017 60

CHAPTER FOUR 63

February 2016 63

The 1960s 65

July 18, 1966 65

Cleveland, 1967 69

Cleveland, 1969 69

Fall, 1995 71

1998 75

Fall 1995 76

CHAPTER FIVE 87

April 26, 2018 87

Fall, 1989 88

April 26, 2018 89

November, 1996 89

April 26, 2018 90

Fall, 2000 90

April 26, 2018 91

August, 2003 91

June, 2004 92

August, 2011 92

July, 2015 93

March, 2016 94

April 26, 2018 95

April, 2016 95

August 11, 2016 96

CHAPTER ONE

Taetrece Ann Harrison

"CHALLENGER"

January 30, 2018

W*e stood in the hallway outside of the courtroom anxiously waiting for a sign that this nightmare would be over. What seemed like hours was fewer than twenty minutes. The jurors had reached a verdict…*

September 28, 2017

After an all-day legal seminar ended, I came out to find my car booted. While I was on the phone to get someone out to remove the boot from my car, I noticed a man across the street walking toward me, but I thought little of it. But while on the phone, I got an eerie feeling like I was being watched. I turned around and the man who had been walking on the opposite side of the street was now so close that he could have kissed me. The man was about my height, dressed in all black clothing including the backpack he was carrying. His clothes were filthy, and I assumed that he was homeless. I was startled by his strange behavior, but I remained calm, although in my mind I was screaming. I thought of various scenarios, but I knew it was best not to appear frightened of the man or his actions.

I stepped back from him, hoping that ignoring him would cause him to move on, but I remained watchful of his movements. Unfortunately, ignoring the stranger was not working; he began talking, but I did not understand his words because I was on the phone. I assumed that the man would take the hint and leave, but instead he kept talking. Although I would not engage in conversation with him or pay him any attention, he continued harassing me while ignoring my subtle hints to leave me alone. Finally, I heard him say something like he has a friend that removes boots from cars. I finally told him that I was fine and that he should leave me alone. It became evident that he was not going to leave me alone, and I realized that my safety was in jeopardy.

By this time, I had managed to return to my car and I opened the driver side door to put some distance between myself and the strange man and to indicate that I was not interested in the continued intrusion. Unfortunately, the man kept moving towards me, even while I was standing inside the open car door, and he was still talking though I was not listening. All my efforts of ignoring him, of not engaging in any way and using my cell phone did not work, so I became more aggressive by raising my voice and tone. I repeated the plea to leave me alone about four times. The strange man began getting agitated when he realized that I was not backing down to this unwanted behavior. He began yelling and cursing by saying, "You fucking bitch!" and "that's why your car has a boot on it!" As he exclaimed these profanities, he finally began slowly walking away towards the intersection of Loyola Avenue and Girod Street. He kept yelling and cursing me as he continued walking away, but suddenly he disappeared between some cars parked to the left of my vehicle. I immediately got a sick feeling in my stomach and realized this encounter was not over. As I looked for the man, and accepted that he was not going away, I firmly announced that I had a firearm and it was best that he moved along. As I yelled out to him, I simultaneously retrieved my firearm from the side compartment of my open driver-side door and placed the semi-automatic on top of the dashboard in my vehicle.

The strange man began to retreat from the parking area and crossed the street. Just as I felt some sense of relief, he returned and began yelling and screaming more obscenities. He taunted me "You don't have a gun and if you then shoot me".

My mind was gripped with fear but I prepared to defend myself if the man decided to follow through on his threats. As quickly as he reappeared, he finally departed the area, but he was still screaming and yelling at me as he was leaving. Despite being very shaken by the whole ordeal I managed to call my sister, Schalyece, and I explained what had just transpired. A parking representative appeared almost immediately after this and removed the two boots from my car and left the parking lot. I headed down Loyola Avenue towards Mid-City, and I noticed that the strange man was still in the area. He was pacing while talking on his cell phone.

Although I was very shaken by the incident, I was volunteering at the debate for mayoral candidates that night, located at WYES television studio in City Park. My emotions were running high, so I figured that talking about it would help me calm myself. I saw my colleague, Nelita Manego Ramey, who was also volunteering for that night's debate, and I decided to tell her what happened, despite still being frightened by the ordeal. Once I explained what happened, I felt it was best to forget about it, and act as if everything was fine, although I was still freaked out.

October 9, 2017

It was Monday morning around 8:30 a.m. when a loud knock rang throughout the house, as I was getting dressed before heading out to pick up a friend. I yelled out for whoever it was to wait a few minutes. As I opened the door, I met five police officers dressed in tactical gear, all holding their guns in a ready position. They asked if I was Taetrece Harrison, to which I replied "Yes." Also, I asked, "What is happening?" They did not respond to this question, but asked if they could come inside while announcing that I was under arrest. My repeated inquiries about the arrest were ignored, while the officers talked among themselves. An officer placed me in handcuffs. I asked several times why was I being arrested. I was escorted outside in handcuffs while my neighbor, Donna Roche, and others from by block, watched as I was placed in the back seat of the police car. Once I was inside the police car, I learned that I was being arrested for the incident two weeks earlier. The stranger had called the police and reported that I pointed a gun at him, and without any investigation, I was on my way to jail.

I had only been to Orleans Parish Prison, otherwise known as OPP, to visit clients, but I'd never been inside the jail itself. Being processed as a criminal defendant was surreal as an attorney. Once I entered OPP, I was not allowed to use my cell phone anymore; it was an end to my independence of doing whatever I wanted.

I had to turn over all personal items, and sit in a holding area for further processing. I was sent to different areas and asked a variety of questions. There was one set of people who asked for personal information such as my name, address, occupation, etc. There was another set of people who took mugshot pictures and fingerprints. Yet another set of people asked medical questions. I tuned out everyone and everything that was going on because the jail setup was geared to break a person down, but I had a strong sense of self. My strength would not allow me to subscribe to any notion of weakness. I felt like the whole process was a complete violation of my rights, and I was ready to leave this foolishness.

October 12, 2017

My thoughts the last three days were of the incident and my arrest, but today was a special day; all bad thoughts were placed on hold. Today, was my fiftieth birthday, and I planned a low-key day with family and friends.

I began with breakfast at the Ritz Carlton New Orleans with my sister, Schalyece, and my best friend, Jacque. After breakfast, Jacque and I decided to do something fun, and we went to a find a trampoline place. On the way, I received an unexpected call from a reporter. They were calling about the arrest on Monday and wanted a statement. I terminated the call and 15 minutes later received another from a new reporter. My milestone birthday had now become a media frenzy, and the day ended with my arrest being talked about all over social media.

October 12, 1967

I was born and raised in New Orleans, Louisiana. New Orleans is divided into wards, and I grew up in Uptown. The wards represent voting sections throughout the city. However, for residents of New Orleans, wards represent much more. It's a New Orleans thing. Growing up in New Orleans means that you identify with the ward you belong to, and each ward carries with it either respect or dismissal. I grew up in the 17th Ward, which contains several different neighborhoods. My street was Leonidas and Olive in Hollygrove, where there was a diversity of races, and people of various backgrounds. While Hollygrove had a reputation for being a rough neighborhood, my block was safe and quiet because everyone knew each other.

My first school experience began at Head Start, which provided a solid foundation for my entire education. Next, I attended Robert E. Lee Elementary School, but I ultimately graduated from St. Joan of Arc Catholic School. My next education experience was when I attended high school at St. Mary's Academy. I was not a match for the all-girl school, and so attended John McDonogh (also known as John Mac) High. Life at John McDonogh was not easy at first as I was constantly teased as being the "Catholic School Girl"; however, I eventually made some friends and life got better. I always talked about going to college then law school, so after graduation I enrolled at the University of Southwestern Louisiana, also known as U.S.L.

My time at U.S.L. abruptly ended because I got married and moved to Washington. My husband was in the military, which meant we moved numerous times. The constant moving made it difficult for my college education, but eventually my husband ended his military career and we settled in Colorado.

I enrolled in college and earned an Associate of Applied Science in Business Management. Then, in May of 1995, I earned a Bachelor of Science in Business Administration from Regis University. I was proud of myself for not giving up on my dreams of being a college graduate. I was inspired to continue my education and looked at attending law school; however, ten years would go by before that would happen.

January, 2000

After living in Colorado for ten years, I wanted to return to the south and settled on moving to Dallas, Texas. I landed a job at a law firm that specialized in foreclosures. While working at the law office, I realized that I still wanted to go to law school. I decided that my dream of going to law school was still possible and began the process of applying for admission. My husband was not supportive, but I applied to Southern University

Law Center, the same school my sister, Schalyece, had graduated from in 1998. My husband and I separated after I applied to law school. Meanwhile, I was accepted at Southern University Law Center and I moved to Baton Rouge, Louisiana in the fall 2002. I graduated in May 2005. While I was in law school, I filed for divorce and was ready to start a new life.

My accomplishments had finally come to fruition after being on hold for a long time. Although it took twenty years, I credited myself for never giving on up on my dreams and staying true to what I wanted. Although my life consisted of some turns, twists, and many detours and delays, I remained vigilant in my convictions to become an attorney.

There was one more dream that I sought. After practicing law for a few years, I decided to obtain a Masters of Law Degree in Taxation, also known as an LLM. After eighteen months of extensive classes, I graduated in fall 2013, and became a tax attorney.

October - December 2017

The story broke on social media, but there was a difference in how I was portrayed by the *Times-Picayune* compared to the *New Orleans Advocate*. The story that *the Times-Picayune* published about me featured my mugshot and a very slanted version of events, despite a statement from my attorney. Another story posted on the same day, about a white male attorney, Mr. Victor Loraso, who was employed with the Attorney General's office and arrested for distributing child pornography, gave a very different portrayal: he was pictured in a suit, not a mugshot.

The *Times-Picayune* has a history of slanting stories about people of color, especially in comparison to white people who may have been accused or arrested for similar incidents. I was not surprised that the *Times-Picayune* would attempt to portray me as some common criminal and discuss the fact that I was a prior candidate for judge four years earlier.

The information about me being a judge candidate was irrelevant because it was meant to solicit an emotional reaction from the readers, also known as a "Red Herring." They knew I was planning to file for candidacy for judge in 2018 and they knew it would influence readers. The intent was to provide the readers with unnecessary information that has no bearing on the current situation.

The story by *New Orleans Advocate* was completely different. My photo was a professional image of me in a suit, and not a mugshot. The story was more objective, as a reported story should be. The *Advocate* presented all pertinent information about what happened to me.

I was completely overwhelmed because my 50th birthday was overshadowed by news stories online. It seemed unreal that an unknown man harassed me despite my numerous requests to be left alone, all to no avail. I advised him that I had a firearm, and did not use it, but I went to jail.

I was confident that the New Orleans District Attorney's office would dismiss these baseless charges and issue a public apology for the mistake. My attorney and friend, John S. Williams and my best friend and attorney Jaque Esptein went to the District Attorney's office to discuss the situation. We met with District Attorney Leon Cannizzaro, Jr. to explain that the facts, as stated by the stranger, whose name I learned was Rorreckee Bates, were false. We assumed that once Cannizzaro learned that Mr. Bates had harassed me this criminal case against me would be over. I felt the meeting was average, and not as productive as I had hoped. I was left to wait for a decision from the District Attorney's office. About two months later, I would get answers from my meeting with Cannizzaro.

There are many things that I would not mind waiting on, but the anticipation of being falsely charged with a crime that carried a potential ten-year prison sentence was a heavy burden. I was under a great deal of pressure and stress. I completely let everything go. I did not work out for weeks, which is uncharacteristic of me, because I was an avid exerciser and gym-goer. My thoughts were consumed with the possibility that this criminal case could go forward, and the potential scenarios of what could happen to me. My level of experience with criminal cases were with misdemeanor crimes such as possession of marijuana, traffic infractions, and other simple crimes. I had no experience with felony cases that required picking a jury.

Furthermore, discussing the situation with people was not in my best interest. There was only one person who I could to, and who I did talk about this disturbing situation with: Jacque. She was there for me from the beginning because we talked about it the day the incident occurred, so she knew everything, even parts that were not revealed in public, or with Cannizzaro. Although I met with Cannizzaro hoping to end this ordeal, my instincts told me that he could not be trusted. This later proved to be true.

December 13, 2017

Clearly, I was misguided in my hope in Cannizzaro's office, because aggravated assault charges were accepted and the criminal case against me was moving forward, to my dismay. I thought back to my meeting with Cannizzaro, as I explained what really had happened, and not the fabricated version told by Mr. Bates. Unfortunately, I foolishly believed that the meeting with Mr. Cannizzaro would yield positive results. My conversation with Cannizzaro was meant to clear up the inconsistencies in the police report. Instead, everything I stated during our meeting was used against me to justify the charges. All attempts to get criminal charges dismissed were constantly ignored by an ineffective Cannizzaro.

I surmised that my 2nd Amendment right to bear arms was non-existent. It was evident to me that, had I been a white female attorney approached by the same person and had I called the police, he would have been arrested—case closed. A white female attorney would have been afforded the benefit of the doubt, that she was defending herself, whereas a black woman attorney would be viewed as the aggressor.

I had to prepare to fight this ridiculous case and determine who was the best attorney to represent me. Deciding on an attorney had to be strategic, since I could get ten years in prison if I was convicted. The process of finding an attorney to represent me should have been easy. However, it was not, because I had to consider numerous factors before making a final selection: gender, race, experience, relationship with the District Attorney's office, relationship with the court, and many other factors.

After talking to several colleagues, I hired Eusi Phillips. Eusi Phillips was a well-known and respected criminal attorney who previously worked at the New Orleans District Attorney's office and had several victories for previous clients. Eusi had all the factors necessary to help me fight this baseless charge. I knew my truth, and with Eusi's expertise I would be victorious. Hiring Eusi offered me relief, and I prepared for an all-out battle against my character, reputation, and veracity. The next few weeks were going to be tense, but I was a woman from Hollygrove who was used to fighting for everything, and this was no different. Besides, I was not going to let Rorreckee Bates or Leon Cannizzaro, Jr. scare or bully me with this foolish criminal matter.

Despite my confidence in my case and Eusi, I still was under a great deal of stress. As an attorney, I knew that anything could happen in a trial and that jurors sometimes get things wrong. Being an attorney, I was trained to look at a problem from both sides. Unfortunately, having the skillset was also a huge downfall because it caused me to be gravely stressed out during the holidays, which I usually love. Also, I withdrew from most people during the holidays, not because I felt like I did something wrong, but because I could not shut my mind down from replaying the incident, and my thoughts about the upcoming trial.

January 4, 2018

My arraignment day. I certainly was not prepared to walk into Orleans Parish Criminal Court on Tulane Avenue and Broad. I walked into the courtroom and saw my name listed on a docket as a Defendant. While Eusi and I waited for my case to be called by the judge, the Assistant District Attorney asked to speak with Eusi. After their conversation, Eusi pulled me out in the hallway to advised me that the District Attorney was offering a "deal." The District Attorney offered to reduce the criminal charge from a felony to a misdemeanor of disturbing the peace. I profoundly said "Hell no." I would not accept any "deal"; I would only accept a dismissal of all charges. Eusi and I had previously agreed that a speedy trial was the best option, and we planned to go forward with this plan. We returned to the courtroom and Judge Karen Herman called my case. The Assistant District Attorney explained that their office had offered a reasonable deal and thought I was planning to accept it. Instead, Eusi entered in my plea of "Not Guilty" and asked for a speedy trial. Judge Herman and the Assistant District Attorney both seemed surprised that I did not accept the misdemeanor for disturbing the peace. Despite their shock, Eusi pushed forward and my trial was scheduled for January 30, 2018 at 9:00 a.m. I was pleased, because in less than three weeks this ordeal would finally be over, and people would know what really happened on September 28, 2017.

I also qualified as a judicial candidate on the same day as my arraignment, in the same building: Orleans Parish Criminal Court. On the first floor, I was seeking to be elected judge so that I could continue to help my community, while, on the second floor, I was fighting for my freedom and my reputation. It was well-known that I was going to run for judge and qualify as a candidate before this nightmare began. I would let nothing deter me from running for judge including this frivolous criminal case.

January 30, 2018

The day of judgment was finally here. I began the day like I always do, by praying and meditating. Although I had meditated, my mind was racing with thousands of thoughts about what could or could not happen. I kept imagining that Cannizzaro was planning to stall the trial by asking for a continuance or use some bluffing tactic to deny me justice.

I arrived at the courthouse, which looked like a dark building full of unknown outcomes. I walked up the steps with my head held high because I knew that today was the end of my nightmare. I arrived on the second floor and walked down the long hallway that echoed with the clacking of my high heels, and I headed toward Division I for Judge Karen Herman's courtroom. As I entered the courtroom, it was surprising to see two court reporters, one from *Times-Picayune* and another from *The New Orleans Advocate*. Another observer was Judge Karen Herman's husband, Stephen J. Herman. I found this quite odd because Stephen J. Herman is a partner at his own firm, and he clearly had nothing pending in his wife's court, and he was not known to handle criminal cases. Nonetheless, I was concerned with my supporters: my mother, my sister Schalyece, Jacque, and the colleagues and friends who came to support me throughout the trial.

The trial began with the selection of jurors. The prospective jurors were escorted in and seated in the jury box area. Each juror was required to state her or his name, their occupation, marital status, and any other pertinent information deemed necessary to gain insight into the person. After the process was done, we gathered in Judge Herman's chambers to determine who we would choose to be on the jury panel. Picking the right juror is a strategic undertaking and entails many factors, such as if juror is a woman or man, their relationship with the police, their level of education, and their experience with the criminal system. After a few hours of talking, questioning, and eliminating, we finally had a jury of six people to hear my case. I was familiar with every process in court, but it seemed like I was watching a movie, except there were no actors, and only real people, and one of them was me.

Once the jurors were selected and sworn in, the trial began with Assistant District Attorneys Hilary Khoury and Inga Petrovich calling witnesses. The first witness was Chantelle Davis, the only detective that handled the case. Detective Davis testified that besides Rorreckee Bates's statement, there were no other witnesses or evidence. Her testimony was very short. When Eusi questioned Davis, she testified that besides taking the statement from Bates, there was no further investigation into his allegations.

The final witness by the state was Rorreckee Bates.

Bates stood up as his name was called to take the witness stand. As he made the short walk from his seat toward the front of the court room, I noticed he was dressed in a dark suit jacket and dress pants. I barely recognized him because I could only see the clothes he wore from the incident when he looked like a homeless man with a dirty black t-shirt and pants and a filthy black backpack. I felt he was faking who he really was for the jurors.

Inga Petrovich began by asking Bates where he lived and worked, and if he was married. Bates said that he lived in Kenner, which is suburb outside of New Orleans, and that he worked as a sound tech at the Hyatt Regency downtown. He answered that he was married and pointed to his wife in the courtroom. Petrovich next asked about what happened on September 28, 2017. Bates began his story by stating he approached me with an offer to help but I told to him to leave me alone and that I went crazy, grabbed my gun, and pointed it at him. Bates said that he ran away, scared, and called 911 for help. Once Petrovich ended her questions for Bates, it was Eusi's turn to ask questions.

There were several things that Eusi planned to solicit when questioning Bates. First, there was a review of the 911 call. Eusi asked Bates to explain why his call lasted almost ten minutes, lacking any sense of urgency after having a gun pointed at him. Bates could not provide any reasonable answers to the questions. Bates fidgeted as the questions became harder and harder for him to provide a straightforward answer. Bates' smug demeanor crumbled each time Eusi asked a new question, and Bates failed to give a reasonable explanation for his story changing as he testified.

Eusi went over Bates's testimony and asked if his version of the facts was truthful and he replied "Yes." Then his 911 call was played in the courtroom while everyone listened. During the call, Bates could be heard asking the operator "what should I do because I need to get to work?" Then, oddly, he kept saying that he was a "football field away from the parking lot." Also, Bates rambled to himself, and there were several pauses while he was on the call. The 911 call lasted over eight minutes. Eusi asked Bates several questions about why the call lasted so long, why he kept asking the operator what to do, and why he seemed so calm and matter-of-fact while saying what happened to him. Also, Eusi asked why there was no sense of urgency while talking to the operator. Bates failed to provide any direct answers, and he repeatedly changed his story regarding the call.

Next, Eusi asked Bates to describe what happened. He reiterated that he asked to help me and that I went crazy and I pointed a snub-nose gun at him. Eusi asked if I was on my cell phone and Bates said "No." Bates testified that he was in the Marines and was familiar with different types of firearms. Eusi got Bates to say several times that I was never on the phone and that he did not see any cell phone. While Eusi continued to ask Bates question after question, his testimony kept changing. Eusi pointed out his inconsistent statements and each time Bates gave a different answer.

In fact, Mr. Bates gave a very different narrative about the incident, stating that I was waiving the gun around, trying to shoot everyone in the area. According to Bates, everyone was in danger because of me waving my firearm in the air. Eusi asked Bates to point out that in his almost 10-minute 911 call, and in his interview with the police officers, all the subsequent statements to the District Attorney's office, and in his earlier testimony, he never stated that I was waiving a gun in the air. Eusi got Bates to agree that this was a new set of facts and it was his first time telling this version of the alleged incident. As Bates kept changing his story, jurors rolled their eyes, shook their heads, and laughed as Bates kept changing the facts about what happened.

The Assistant District Attorneys ended their case without ever producing a snub-nose gun alleged by Rorreckee Bates or the two police officers who responded to the 911 call. The Assistant District Attorneys' case solely rested with Rorreckee Bates and no other witnesses or evidence.

Eusi's strategy was to call the best witness who could relay what really happened. He called me as a witness. Although I was very nervous to testify, I was confident in my truth about how things really happened on September 28, 2017. I finally would tell my side of the story.

Eusi began by asking some general questions about myself, such as where was I born, what schools had I attended, and what my profession was, and the type of cases I handled. He then asked about what I was doing on September 28, 2017. I explained that I attended the all-day legal seminar that ended at 5:00 p.m. I recounted how I walked to my car to discover that it was booted, and that I immediately called the company to have it removed.

Eusi introduced my cell phone records as evidence. These were key in my case, and proof that Bates had been lying from the outset. However, the Assistant District Attorneys objected to the use of my cell phone data without a representative from Sprint being present. Then, Eusi argued that it was my phone records; therefore, I could testify about my phone calls. Unfortunately, Judge Herman disagreed with my attorney's argument and would not allow my cell phone records introduced as evidence. But, Eusi and I are both great lawyers because we knew the key to any problem is knowing another option and we worked around this minor setback.

Eusi and I successfully got my phone records admitted by what is legally called "recall of memory." Eusi asked if I recalled what time I placed my call to remove the boot from my car, and I said that I didn't remember. Eusi asked that, if he showed me my cell bill and I saw the time, would that jog my memory, and I said "Yes." Then, Eusi had me look at my cell phone bill and asked me to state out loud the time of the call. Eusi and I were able to prove, through the recall of memory process, that I was on my phone from the time that I arrived at my vehicle until the time I left the parking lot. I also testified on what type of phone I had, which was an IPhone 7 Plus in an Otterbox case. Furthermore, I testified that I held my phone in my dominant hand which is my right hand, and the Iphone 7 Plus was very large and heavy.

Eusi next questioned me concerning my gun. He asked if I owned a snub-nose firearm. I replied that "I own a semiautomatic." Eusi asked if I knew what a snub-nose gun was, and I replied, "Yes, a snub-nose gun is a revolver which has a cylinder, and I have a semi-automatic which had a clip." The jurors listened intently as I revealed what really happened on the night of the incident. I could see the jurors' reactions to my testimony. Everyone was attentive and listening as I spoke about the incident.

Petrovich began her cross examination, going over my testimony and asking if I was angry about my car having a boot. I responded, "No, because I made a mistake and the parking time had expired." I also stated, "That, I had my car booted before for time expiring, so I was familiar with the process and it was no big deal." Next, Petrovich asked if I was upset because I had plans to go out drinking with friends and the boot was causing me to be late. I explained, "I never testified that I was going out with friends and I do not drink." Petrovich seemed surprised when I said that I did not drink. She quickly had to ask something different, because it was obvious that she was not prepared for my response. Just as Petrovich was about to take her seat, she popped back up and asked one more question. She asked if I was running for judge. Eusi objected to the question, but I saw the look of shock on the jurors' faces, and some of them gasped. I was instructed by Judge Herman to respond to her question. I replied "Yes, I am a candidate for judge in the upcoming election."

The testimony portion of the trial was finally over. Next, each attorney gave a closing argument before the jurors met to decide an outcome.

Eusi's closing argument was, "Why Are We Here?" He went on to say that the Assistant District Attorney gave the answer when she asked if I was running for judge. It was no secret that I was planning to run for judge when the incident occurred in 2017. Eusi reminded the jurors that Bates said that I was never on my phone and never saw a phone. Eusi stated that we proved that was not truthful based on all my phone calls. Additionally, Eusi argued that the Assistant District Attorney never brought forth any firearm, any additional witnesses, no video, nor any other evidence to prove what Bates had stated during the trial. Eusi pointed out that Detective Davis was called as witness, that she only testified what was repeated by Bates, but that she personally did not conduct any investigation into his allegations. Eusi again said "Why Are We Here?" and asked the jurors to reach a verdict of not guilty.

The Assistant District Attorney gave her closing argument, but it was a carbon copy of Bates' testimony. Again, she stated that I was angry, but she had no evidence to prove that except for speculation. Finally, she said that because I was running for judge, I would say anything not to go to jail.

Judge Herman gave the jurors instructions and they went to the back to discuss. A deputy came outside in the hallway and said the jurors had reached a verdict. I prepared myself as I walked back inside the courtroom.

The jurors had taken less than twenty minutes to decide. The juror handed a folded paper with their response, and the deputy handed this to Judge Herman. She asked me to stand and she read the verdict "Not guilty." I let out a huge sigh of relief and dropped my head and said thank you to God for a victory. This horrible nightmare was truly over, and the jurors saw the truth. As the verdict was read, Petrovich exclaimed, "I can't fucking believe it."

I turned to her and said, "You ought to be ashamed of yourself for putting me and my family through this." We left the courtroom and I returned home but I was mentally exhausted from the incident, from the months of waiting, from the trial, and lastly by the verdict. Despite my weak mental state, I prayed and thanked God all night for seeing me through this situation.

I had hoped that it would have been easy to just move on after the verdict, but it was not so easy for life to return to normal. I continued to have sleepless nights while replaying the trial over and over in my dreams. I began watching everyone when I parked my car in downtown New Orleans. I began meditating to help calm my mind and my restlessness.

I had fought bullies named Leon Cannizzaro and Rorreckee Bates. I stood up when most people would have felt defeated. I did not waiver because that was never an option. I faced the danger of losing my life to a possible ten-year sentence. I refused to run and hide. I stood up for all women who may face someone like Rorreckee Bates and other injustices that black women must endure. I stood in my truth because I needed the next woman to know that she needs to know that being a victim is not an option, but being a champion for herself is possible because I did it.

I stood up against what, to most, may seem impossible: a bully, the ongoing less-than treatment of women, especially women of color. I stood for those women who are too afraid to do something for themselves, for women who do not have the resources to fight back, for those little girls who will one day become women. I stand against those who think women should not fight back, and I stand up for women who continue to be oppressed by men. I stand for the number one: for myself and the truth.

CHAPTER TWO

DESIRÉE M. CHARBONNET

"ACHIEVER"

W hen the lights turned off at the end of her last day, it marked the close of ten years at court. Memories of those years flashed by, but a few things came into clear focus. Just a year earlier she'd earned national recognition for exceptional advocacy work, and she'd recently announced a quest to become a candidate for judge at the court of appeals. But her love for her city and her desire to be an integral part in making it better were more important, and this caused her to shift focus. However, a big question remained to be answered: would the city love her back?

Desirée Mary Charbonnet was a bright and beautiful little girl, with a vibrant smile. She was born and raised in New Orleans, Louisiana. Desirée is also considered a "Creole" descendant of New Orleans. She grew up in a neighborhood called "Gentilly" which residents also referred to as the "Seventh Ward". Gentilly's name was derived from a plantation dating back to 1727. Although, Gentilly began as a place where slaves were forced to work, it ultimately became known as the "Creole" neighborhood.

The term "Creole" refers to people of mixed race who were born in Louisiana during the French and Spanish periods. Creole families started occupying Gentilly as early as the 1700s. The influx of Creoles eventually made up most of the residents in Gentilly, and this continued for decades. Houses in Gentilly were like the California bungalow style, unlike familiar shot-gun style homes in New Orleans that are mostly found in the French Quarter and in the Uptown neighborhoods. These bungalows lined Virgil Blvd, which kids shortened to simply, "The Blvd".

As kids played outside, the aroma of creole cooking filled the block. The Blvd was home to mostly middle-class families, with two parents working to maintain a sensible lifestyle. Parents sacrificed because education was hugely important. Parents felt the only proper place to obtain an education was in private school, and not just any private school, but Catholic schools. Uniforms were the usual attire worn through the week, while the weekends welcomed kids by allowing them to wear anything but a white button-down shirt.

Among Creole families there were long-standing traditions handed down from generation to generation. A few prevalent traditions were the importance of a good education and striving to be your best. These beliefs continued to resonate over the decades and passed from family to family. Desirée's parents were diligent about instilling in her the importance of a good education, doing her best, and maintaining her faith in God.

Desirée's first good educational experience was at St. Leo the Great Elementary School. St. Leo The Great provided the same values her parents taught her, which continued when she went to high school, and graduated from Cabrini High School. While Cabrini could be a challenging school, it further helped establish in Desirée a foundation for working hard to succeed. The four years of high school went by quickly, and Desirée was thrilled to begin a new chapter in her life. She had dreams of being successful after finishing high school, and she knew that to reach those goals going to college was the necessary path.

Desirée was smart and ready for the vigorous tasks that college, then later law school, would pose. She earned her bachelor's degree and her law degree from Loyola University in New Orleans, and she was much closer to her goal of being successful.

Desirée worked as an attorney and enjoyed helping others with their problems. But she wanted to do more than just help a few people. She looked at politics as a way to make a difference for the entire city of New Orleans. She made her first political run for Recorder of Mortgages in New Orleans in 1998. Most candidates do not win their first race because voters are unfamiliar with the new candidate, but Desirée was not most candidates. Desirée won her first political race against an incumbent, and she made history by becoming the first woman elected as Recorder of Mortgages in Orleans Parish.

Desirée believed in serving the public by providing information that could be useful for improving their lives. While working as Recorder of Mortgages she commenced a program that taught renters about becoming homeowners. She wanted people to know the importance of being a homeowner which would improve their lives, as well as the city's economy. She maintained the position of Recorder of Mortgages for almost ten years, at which point she began to pursue another political seat.

In 2007, Desirée became a candidate for Judge at Municipal Court in New Orleans. She easily won and became Judge Desirée Mary Charbonnet. She again made history by becoming the first woman judge elected at Municipal Court, since the court began electing judges in 1948. Desirée was destined to keep making history, because five years later, she became the first female Chief Judge at Municipal Court.

As a judge, Desirée continued to be essential by implementing a diversion program for non-violent defendants. She recognized that there were better options than just sending people to jail. In 2016, she earned accolades from the National Association of Women Judges and other legal entities for her innovative approach to the resolution of prostitution and human trafficking cases that came into her court. Later, in December 2016, Desirée announced that she would seek to fill the vacated seat at New Orleans Fourth Circuit Court of Appeals by becoming a candidate. Based on her past political wins, it was predicted that Desirée would win the race. However, a few months later, Desirée would be a candidate in a different political race. She embarked on an unexpected journey.

It had been rumored for a few months that Desirée was interested in running for Mayor of New Orleans; however, these rumors were dismissed as wishful thinking. The resounding response was that a plan was set in motion for her to run for another judge seat, and not for mayor. Yet things changed rapidly, because on May 23, 2017, Desirée announced her candidacy for mayor. As a judge there are rules that prevented Desirée from revealing her plans to run for mayor, so she officially resigned as Chief Judge of Municipal Court on April 21, 2017. She made her formal announcement before her family, friends and supporters, marking the beginning of a new chapter in her political career. Desirée hoped to make history again by becoming the first female mayor of New Orleans in the city's 300 years of existence.

Mayor of New Orleans is a coveted position, so it was not surprising that eighteen candidates, including Desirée, entered the race. By this time, Desirée had been in the political arena for almost twenty years, so it was not surprising that she was considered a front-runner, along with City Councilwoman, LaToya Cantrell, and retired Judge Michael Bagneris. But Desirée was deemed the lead candidate and predicted winner from the beginning.

As soon as she became a candidate for mayor, Desirée also became a target by most of the candidates, as well as various well-known political operatives in New Orleans. In fact, out of the eighteen candidates for mayor, Desirée was targeted by negative media campaigns the most because she posed the largest threat to the other candidates. Attacking another candidate is not the best strategy, but many believed it to be an effective tactic. Despite many voters' disapproval of attacks, candidates still use these methods in the hopes of winning. Attacks on candidates are not unusual, but most attacks are typically launched a few days before the actual election day, in order to limit the other side from responding; therefore, the damage is already done to the opponent. But the attacks against Desirée began very early, and they increased throughout the entire campaign.

The first attack against Desirée began with media reports of her missing mayoral candidate forums. Although it is not unusual for a candidate to be absent at a forum, media reporting of the incidents caused a frenzy, and any absences drew strong condemnation. However, when other candidates were absent at various events, there was virtually no media coverage. The media coverage surrounding Desirée's absences was one of the most discussed topics throughout the campaign, and this was constantly questioned by many voters. Although Desirée's appearances at many forums outnumbered her absences, the news media focused only on the negative.

The next attack on Desirée was direct and personal and came from Sidney Torres. Sidney grew up in St. Bernard Parish, which is about thirty-six to forty-five miles outside of New Orleans. Most people in New Orleans consider anyone who grew up outside of the city to be an outsider, and not an authority on all things New Orleans. Nonetheless, Sidney Torres is a real estate developer in New Orleans, and he gained recognition after Hurricane Katrina when he used his company, SDT Waste and Debris, to aid in hurricane clean-up efforts around the city. Sidney continued to maintain his popularity because of the waste company and real estate development around New Orleans. Rumors circled around the city that Sidney was planning to run for mayor, and some residents delighted in the idea. Nevertheless, shortly before the election, he announced that he would not seek the seat for mayor.

Despite Sidney's decision not to enter the mayoral race, he decided to become involved with the election as a concerned citizen. This concern over the election took the form of a media-driven political action committee named The VOICE PAC. The intention was to help ensure that that the incoming mayor offered viable solutions to the voters. Sidney, through The VOICE PAC, scheduled a debate forum for September 27, 2017. Although there were eighteen candidates for mayor, invitations were sent to the four top candidates for mayor only. The forum was well advertised to guarantee that many voters and spectators would be in attendance for the event.

Desirée was among the four candidates invited to the VOICE PAC forum, and it was confirmed that she would attend the event. However, a few days before the scheduled event, Desirée's campaign office released a statement sighting various reasons for declining to attend. Initially, Sidney's criticisms of Desirée's absence appeared to come from a concern citizen; however, after a few days it was evident that it was intended as a personal attack. Desirée's withdrawal from the debate ignited a series of unprecedented anti-Desirée advertisements, including disparaging commercials aired during a New Orleans Saints game to ensure the message got out to voters. This one-person crusade was a direct attack on Desirée's character, with a goal to destroy her campaign for mayor.

Desirée is a person who can withstand any type of situation because of her long standing experience in politics. She is familiar with handling difficult people when working as a judge. She recognized the bullying tactics, and they appeared to be rants by a person who clearly had a hidden agenda. She maintained her position on declining to attend the debate, and would not waver on her choice. However, after days and days of mudslinging by Sidney, Desirée's campaign office sent a letter calling for his actions to cease. Ultimately, the response appeared to be unnoticed, because voters were constantly gossiping about Sidney's negative statements about Desirée.

The third attack against Desirée emanated from another newly formed political action group named NOT For Sale NOLA. The group was formed by influential business people from New Orleans and Baton Rouge, all of them with deep pockets. Their agenda was simple: make sure that Desirée would not become Mayor of New Orleans, by using whatever they deemed necessary to reach that goal. First, the group began with offensive and demeaning commercials like Sidney's, except these included a racist cartoon of Desirèe. The next approach was more aggressive, and came in the form of a character assassination in mailers sent to predominately white voters to gain their support. The mailers were called *The Desirée Charbonnet Tales*, and included a depiction of a racist and sexist cartoon character based on Desirée. The mailers promised to expose people Desirée was affiliated with in her campaign. However, none of the mailers addressed anything about Desirée or her almost twenty years in politics. The subsequent mailer was named *Chapter 2, Desirée and her Krewe of Cronies*. Here was another cartoon depiction of Desirée, this time wearing a hat and uniform and holding a large firearm. Additionally, this group produced a different mailer of fake money with Desirée's picture on the bill, along with the phrase *Pay to Play Desirée*.

The cartoon imagery of Desirée were direct replays from Jim Crow-era caricatures used to project an image of buffoonery and mockery of a black woman. It was meant to cause her demise as a black female, and to destroy her character and countless accomplishments over the last twenty years of service to the citizens of New Orleans. Desirée was alarmed by the second attacks because the tactics were equally offensive as the earlier attacks, but with racist overtones. She was irritated that a group of people would submit themselves to this type of behavior. Regardless of these deliberate personal attacks, she would not deter from her campaign. She was more determined than ever to continue getting her message out to the voters, and to prove who she really was. She felt it was easier for the group to make allegations against her, than it was to direct any attention to her spotless record of

20 years. She viewed the attacks as distractions meant to sway voters, and all of them based on things irrelevant to the election.

The next attack came directly from at least one opponent, Michael Bagneris. Michael is a native of New Orleans, and a former Civil District Court Judge. He resigned after twenty years on the bench in December 2013, with the hopes of unseating incumbent Mitch Landrieu. Michael's campaign had a short timeframe in which to make an impact on voters: fewer than forty-five days before the election. But election night on February 1, 2014 proved to be unsuccessful for Michael because incumbent Mayor Mitch Landrieu was declared the winner. Now, Michael was seeking a second chance to become Mayor of New Orleans, and he was one of the four top contenders. Just like Michael had done four years ago, Desirée had resigned from a position as judge. Desirée and Michael were the two candidates who had the most similar backgrounds; they were both natives of New Orleans, both were attorneys, and both were former judges. One would assume them to be allies and not opponents in the race for mayor.

Mayoral debates are usually an excellent time for the audience to see what a person is about and to learn about their ideas to make the city better. The mayoral debates would typically have a stage for the candidates to sit or stand on while a moderator asked various questions while an audience of supporters, news reporters, voters, and various others observed. In the lead up to the election, almost every night there was a debate hosted by various organizations around the city to provide voters an opportunity to determine who they should support as the next mayor. Getting to know the candidates was an important process for voters to make an informed decision.

Night after night during each debate, voters began to witness at least one candidate's character and demeanor on display. Desirée was considered the candidate to beat which made her a target, and debates are ideal places for other candidates to highlight themselves for voters. Michael had issues with Desirée, which started during the first debate, then became obvious as each debate took place night after night.

During a televised debate, the opponents were asked to say something pleasant about each other. Michael gave excellent compliments to each opponent, yet he reduced his compliment about Desirée to her being a fashionable dresser. Likewise, at another filmed debate, Michael offered pleasantries about each opponent, but again he reduced Desirée to merely wearing nice shoes. During the debates Michael's character and demeanor toward Desirée was on display for everyone to witness and there was a disdain that could not be hidden.

October 14, 2017—Primary Election
Desirée met primary election day with anticipation after

months of campaigning, nightly debates, and fundraising events to garner the support of voters. Once the polls closed the crowded race of eighteen candidates had narrowed to two. The voters had made it abundantly clear that the city was poised for its first female mayor. Latoya Cantrell had received 39% of votes, while Desirée received 37% of votes, coming in second.

In preparation for the next thirty days, which could lead to victory, Desirée's campaign deemed it necessary for voters to get a full impression of Latoya Cantrell's character. Revelations of Latoya's problems came immediately after the primary election. Detailed information about questionable usage of a city-issued credit card became public. Pages and pages of credit card statements listed hundreds of dollars in personal expenses. In addition, it was discovered that Latoya had an outstanding tax lien from the Internal Revenue Service for unpaid taxes. The news about Latoya was alarming and speculation began to circulate that most voters would reconsider changing their support and move to Desirée. Yet, the allegations of Latoya's ethnical issues became a mere trivial matter to most voters, but this was particularly true in the black community. Instead, all the negativity and disdain were directed towards Desirée, even though her twenty-year political career was scandal-free.

Though both Desirée and Latoya were black, there still was a divide within the black community based on

the adage known in New Orleans as being "color struck."
In most cities in the U.S., internal racism is usually called
"colorism." Internal racism among the black community
began as far back as during slavery. Slave owners would
separate blacks based on the lightness or darkness of their
skin, which ultimately pit people with different shades
of skin pigment against each other. Being Color Stuck,
or having Colorism, is an ever-present factor still today
among blacks, hundreds of years later. Desirée was seen
differently by different voters. Many black voters saw
Desirée as privileged, since she had attended a private
high school and college. Most black voters presumed that,
because of her lighter skin color, she was automatically
offered advantages in her life. However, most white
voters saw Desirée as a person who worked hard and had
made something of herself. The white voters deemed her
a person who overcame obstacles by attending college
and law school.

Although both Desirée and LaToya worked hard
to achieve their goals, the mayoral race became one
about a lighter complexioned candidate versus a darker
complexioned candidate. Basically, any comparison of
Desirée to LaToya was invariably favorable for LaToya
to many black voters, even though Desirée's credentials
outweighed Latoya's in every aspect. Desirée was a
lifelong resident of New Orleans. She had more years
of education. Her twenty years of serving the citizens of
New Orleans with a spotless record resulted in her being

nationally recognized for her outstanding work, and implementation of beneficial programs for the betterment of others. And she had a history of a temperament capable of handling any situation. On the other hand, Latoya had grown up in Compton, California. During her capacity as city councilwoman, she voted against a long standing tradition by showing a lack of connection with New Orleans. She had a shorter political resume of only seven years. She was demonstrated to be directly involved in issues of unpaid taxes and improper city-issued credit card usage, and this showed her lack of temperament. Most voters overlooked that Desirée was a native of New Orleans, which previously was a significant factor for voters. That Desirée had been in politics much longer than LaToya, and that she was vocal for her neighborhood after Hurricane Katrina, again, this was not an important factor for voters as it concerned Desirée.

November 18, 2017-Election Day

Ultimately, election day arrived and Desirée M. Charbonnet was defeated, and LaToya Cantrell made history by becoming the first black female mayor of New Orleans. The campaign trail had not been easy for Desirée Charbonnet. The path was paved with nothing but daily roadblocks of character attacks. Desirée was the only candidate who had the task of overcoming persistent obstacles placed before her. Although Desirée's road did not lead to victory, she should be commended sacrificing her judicial position for the city she loves so dearly. There are not many who are brave enough to surrender themselves the way Desirée did, for an unknown possibility of a potential victory as mayor. Despite the fact that Desirée was denied the opportunity to make history once again by being the first black female mayor, she undoubtedly has proven that she is an amazing person who can endure all criticism and still be a phenomenal woman.

Recently, Desirée opened the Law Office of Desirée M. Charbonnet, proving that she is a person who can reinvent herself and do anything she focuses on. Although Desirée is no longer in public office, she continues to serve the community by sitting as Ad Hoc Judge for her fellow colleagues at Orleans Parish Municipal and Traffic Courts. Desirée is also a person who should be admired for having the tenacity to still stand and serve the community in a different capacity as a knowledgeable attorney for the citizens of New Orleans.

All the attacks came down to not liking Desirée's potential for greatness at being Mayor of New Orleans. Each group made claims against her about her associations, but nothing was ever stated about her stellar reputation for working tirelessly on behalf of others' betterment. Those are qualities of a true leader, and a person who should oversee the work of continuing to make New Orleans great. Desirée presented her authentic self during the campaign, but many chose to believe the lies instead of seeing the truth before them. Voters have a right to choose their candidate, but in this election, a candidate was chosen for them, while another was berated out of mere jealousy.

CHAPTER THREE

GAY POLK PAYTON

"DOER"

August 2014

The dismay on Gay's face was reflected in her eyes, as she received notice of a formal grievance about being an embarrassment to the legal profession. Once she finished reviewing each allegation, her clenched jaw and closed fists were signs of her dogged determination to overcome this horrible situation. Gay was appalled, and intended to challenge these falsehoods; otherwise, her life would drastically change and her long-time legal career would be in jeopardy. Gay's tenacity has resonated within her, even while growing up as a little black girl in the Deep South, when at the time it was unfavorable to be vocal as a black person.

1960s

Gay Polk was born in the late 1960s in Hattiesburg, Mississippi, which happens to be nicknamed "Hub City" because of its proximity to major cities such as New Orleans, Jackson, Gulfport, and Mobile. Gay grew up when Hattiesburg was at the center of effecting changes throughout Mississippi as many in the city were helping blacks register to vote during the Civil Rights Movement. The rise of any civil rights movement in Hattiesburg led directly to racial violence against any blacks deemed too vocal for changing segregation.

Despite the rampant violence against blacks in Hattiesburg, change did come because people refused to allow intimidation, fear and racial assaults to sway any attempts of equality. Although Gay was a young child during this time of upheaval for racial equality, she was an impressionable child who learned to speak up against any injustices she witnessed. Most blacks in the south were strong believers in God, and their belief was an integral part in trusting that their lives would get better. Gay's family was immensely involved with church and their belief in God, and those values passed on to her as a little girl. She progressed in learning to trust God and to have faith while leaning on His understanding for her entire life. Her belief in God was absolute, and at the center of Gay's being, which followed her into adulthood. Besides her unwavering faith in God, she realized while attending church that singing was one of her many talents. Little Gay's singing delighted the ears of the congregation as she belted out incredible gospel songs that filled up the church. Gay's singing voice became a major part of her life while growing up, and it continued to flourish over the years.

Although she had a strong affection for singing, she recognized that she possessed many other talents. Gay discovered that she was skillful at negotiations even as a young girl. Whenever, she was due to be punished for being mischievous, her artful talent for compromising to thwart any actions by her parents would successfully earn her a pass from reprimand. Gay's dynamic personality, along with her persistence to speak up against any injustices, augmented her enormous faith in God, and made Gay a fierce black woman-in-the-making. Gay always worked to build a narrative about who she was and what she wanted to become from childhood to adulthood.

1990s

Gay gladly entered college -as the start of a new journey in young adult life. She felt college would provide the opportunity to sharpen her various skills while preparing for the next quest in law school. She completed college with a bachelor's degree in her hometown of Hattiesburg at the University of Southern Mississippi. Thereafter, Gay left Mississippi and continued her educational pursuits to obtain a master's degree at the University of New Orleans. Admittedly, Gay enjoyed her time in New Orleans, but she longed to return home and continue to further herself by attending another college. Gay had prepared for this moment for many years, and finally she enrolled in law school at the University of Mississippi, better known as "Ole Miss." She appreciated being in law school, despite it coming with a tremendous amount of assignments and an extensive amount of stress; she welcomed all challenges from learning about the law. Her perseverance and commitment for doing the best work would contribute throughout her three years of law school. Those three years of grinding hours of studying, classes and exams, all swiftly ended and marked one of her greatest achievements. She graduated, and it was the commencement of her ultimate dream of being an attorney. The excitement of obtaining a law degree only lasted for a short while because Gay had to prepare for one more step before being called Esquire. She had heard the many horror stories while in law school about taking the bar exam, and preparing for this exam would consume all her energy and time over the next few months. After months of preparing and waiting, she received the results: Gay passed the bar exam.

In 1996 she became a Mississippi attorney, and she set out to forge a career by opening a law office.

Gay planned to be an integral part of the community by offering her knowledge and expertise to those who gravely needed it. As a new attorney, she handled a variety of cases, but ultimately criminal cases were her favorite area of the law. Being from the community, she understood the lack of resources and ongoing problems which plagued her clients. Her insight into her clients' problems made her an amazing attorney who was skillful at helping them effectively maneuver through the court system. Gay developed a reputation for being a persistent attorney who fought hard in court on behalf of her clients. Each time she aided a client in the community, she had a sense of gratification because everything possible was done to solve their problems.

2011

Over the course of fifteen years, Gay became a master at multitasking, a skill she learned as a young girl. She practiced the law while maintaining her singing career, as well as many other activities, which made her an impressive woman. Her list of involvements over the years included being a professor, a former president of the local bar association, an active member of the Delta Sigma Theta Sorority, a certified fitness instructor, a blogger, a radio show host, a songwriter, and all while being a single mom.

Gay reflected over her many accomplishments, delighting in achieving most of her childhood dreams.

However, she pondered her next undertaking. Before doing anything, Gay always asked God for guidance in her next opportunity. After much thought, consideration and prayer, she decided to run for judge in the upcoming 2011 election.

Gay formally announced to her community that she was seeking the judge position at Forrest County Justice Center. She was ready to get out into the community and seek the support of the voters. She campaigned throughout the community by expressing to each voter her commitment to them and ensured each case would be handled with fairness. Her campaign consisted of making sure to introduce herself to each voter and asking for support. Her message to the voters was a simple reminder of how she had been serving her community over the last fifteen years and would continue to serve as their judge when they cast a vote for her.

Gay was faithful that she would be successful and realize her dream of becoming a judge. The campaign was exciting, but Gay enjoyed meeting and speaking with the voters in her community the most. Gay campaigned as if she was the only person running for judge and it worked, because a few months later she won with over three thousand votes compared to the other candidates who received only a few hundred votes. Gay was happy to add another title to her long list of roles: Judge Gay Polk-Payton at Forrest County Justice Court. She was excited to be a judge because it meant being able to help more people in the community who needed it.

2012

The beginning of 2012 proved to be an amazing start for Gay. She began the new year filled with joy because all her effort led to her becoming a judge. She was eager to stay dedicated to making a difference in the community. Another benefit of her being a judge, the job was part-time which allowed for handling her legal cases for her clients. She was in the best of both worlds.

Even as Gay settled into understanding how the court operated and her work as a judge, she continued to maintain her many other roles: her singing and songwriting career, and as a blogger. She was in high demand throughout Mississippi to sing her best version of the National Anthem at sporting events. In addition, her original songs, "Real Man" and "God Gives Me," were both featured in the movie soundtrack of *Blackbird (2014, film)*.

Gay combined her desire to help others with writing on her social media accounts, and she wrote her own PSAs, or Public Service Announcements. Her words of wisdom involved details on relationships, health, fitness and legal issues. She believed offering guidance on a variety of subjects would prevent people from any potential mistakes if they were properly informed.

After years of writing various posts on social

media, she contemplated the idea of exposing the daily PSAs to a wider audience beyond Facebook and Twitter. She came to realize that years of offering advice could be useful to many others in the form of a book. She began planning for another new role, that of a published author. Almost two years after becoming a judge, in December 2013, she published her first book, titled *This Is a Public Service Announcement*, which featured Gay wearing her judicial robe on the front cover.

August 4, 2014

It was the beginning of the week with Monday registering ninety-one degrees of scorching heat over downtown Jackson, Mississippi. Downtown was bustling with people heading into various office buildings, trying to avoid the summer heat. Most people hate Mondays because it means the weekend of fun is over and it's time to get back to work. Taking in complaints was a daily occurrence at the Ethics Commission office. Sometime during the day, a package arrived in the mail, with no return address. Inside the package were numerous printouts from someone's social media account and other various screenshots. There was nothing unusual about the *package*, because complaints are sent through the mail as well other ways. There was no letter included with the package; it was merely several printouts regarding a local judge from Forrest County Justice Center. It was clear the anonymous sender had some strong objections to how this local judge had been acting.

The Ethics Commission acts upon complaints brought before its office by investigating. After an investigation is conducted and finds the allegations are true, then formal action is taken against an offending judge. The Ethics Commission conducted a cursory inquiry by reviewing the screenshot printouts from the package and researching online for confirmation. This brief investigation led to a decision that a local judge should be punished immediately.

On Monday, August 4, 2014, the Ethics Commission announced that after checking into Gay's social media accounts and reviewing her book, it was determined that she was behaving badly and using her judicial position for personal gain. The Ethics Commission also indicated that it would act in the form of punishment against Gay, including public embarrassment.

Gay's initial reaction was disbelief that the Ethics Commission thought she did anything wrong, and it was obvious that she was being falsely accused. She immediately felt her name and reputation was being attacked. She had been immersing herself with helping others for many years; these allegations were a shock. She was unable to imagine who would do something to ruin her legal career. Gay considered herself to be a strong person who did not back down from any type of challenge, and she decided that her fight against these allegations would define the narrative of who she truly was in the community. Gay's determination to clear her name would take an exhausting three years before she got her day in court—but not just any court, the Mississippi Supreme Court.

Surprises can bring on immense joy or cause unimaginable pain, and no one knows the outcome until that very moment of a reaction. Sometime in the summer of 2014, Gay received a surprise. The Mississippi State Commission for Judges informed her that the anonymous complaint was with the Mississippi State Commission regarding her singing career, the book cover, and her social media accounts. The complaint alleged that Gay was using her status as a judge for personal gain, and was causing an embarrassment to the legal community and was a violation of conduct for judges. She was very surprised and shocked by the anonymous complaint. But she would not be silent against this injustice.

June 13, 2017

She began her day like usual by sending prayers up to God and expressing gratitude for His wonderful works. However, today she knew would be a long one, so preparing herself in faith and belief was paramount this morning. Despite being in this situation, she remained steadfast that God would lead her to victory over her enemies. Gay Polk-Payton recognized that she was a child of God, and nothing nor no one could prevent her belief in God's goodness, especially not today.

It was a gloomy day, but sunshine was just behind those clouds, ready to brighten up the sky for Gay's big day in court. June 13, 2017 had been coming for months—years—since the controversy started in August 2014. Nonetheless, Gay was focused and ready for the entire ordeal to end, but she understood this was just another step to finally prove that she had done nothing wrong and that her enemies would lose. Although Gay's strength was her faith, waiting was her weakness, but she identified that this one time she had to sit back and let others handle things on her behalf.

The Mississippi Supreme Court has a long history dating back to its inception in 1817, by creation of the first state constitution. The creation of the court was during the height of slavery in the Deep South, of which Mississippi was a central part. The court building is in the west central part of Jackson, the capital city of Mississippi. The history of the Mississippi Supreme Court is very similar to most courts during the slavery and Jim Crow eras, and it was not favorable to blacks who frequently sought relief from racism and severe mistreatments. Currently, the Mississippi Supreme Court is different than its history. The court has always had nine justices, almost all of whom, historically, have been white men. Today, those nine justices are a combination of black and white, with eight men and one woman.

As Gay steered toward Jackson, which was an hour-and-half drive away, she considered the many possible outcomes for the day. However, Gay would not allow negativity to divert her attention, because her focus was on a successful conclusion with the Mississippi Supreme Court. Gay arrived at the courthouse, although it is not the most inviting place. The building stands as a distinguished four-story concrete structure. Appearing in the Supreme Court, Gay felt this was a daunting undertaking, yet it was exhilarating at the same time. Gay entered the building knowing that her life would be different no matter what happened today. Gay arrived on the fourth floor, walked down a long hall and into the courtroom. Gay noticed several people were present; however, her focus remained with why she was there. Gay proceeded toward the first row and sat down directly behind her attorneys. Gay was overwhelmed with anticipation as she tried to patiently wait for the justices to arrive and begin her hearing.

Although it seemed like a lifetime to Gay, the six justices quickly entered the courtroom and her hearing began. As the justices took their seats, it felt like a scene from a movie, except this was not Netflix, but Gay's life on display, being scrutinized by six colleagues. Gay tentatively prepared to listen while the opposing side, Attorney Rachel W. Michel, slowly walked to the microphone to begin spilling out the Ethics Commission's argument that Gay's conduct was an embarrassment to the legal and judicial profession. Michel spoke for about forty minutes to try to sway the justices to agree that Gay was wrong and deserved to be publicly punished. Once Michel was done, it was finally Gay's lawyers' opportunity to express their arguments concerning this situation.

Gay had at least four attorneys who would speak on her behalf against this frivolous anonymous attacker. The judges asked an exhaustive list of questions of all the attorneys, but one question asked was who was the unknown person that filed the complaint against Gay, and what was the person's motivation for doing it? The judges were keenly aware that the unknown person's identity would have been a significant fact, because it appeared to be nefarious in its intent for making these claims against Gay. However, to the dismay of everyone, Michel advised the court that no investigation was undertaken to determine who had filed the accusations against Gay. Michel went on to tell the court that the Ethics Commission simply reviewed the things the unknown caller complained about and agreed with the complainant. That was the extent of their investigation. Gay endured about two hours of listening to all the reasons for and against her social media posts and other actions. Once everything ended, Gay prepared herself to wait several months for a decision, because the Supreme Court had a history of taking a long time—sometimes even a year—to decide on a case.

June 15, 2017

Friday, June 15, 2017 was a hot and humid summer day in Hattiesburg, Mississippi. The city was bustling with folks getting ready for the weekend and kids recently beginning their summer vacations. It was a typical Friday for most people in Hattiesburg, but not for Gay. She had been waiting on a final decision from a three-year ordeal. Although she is woman of enormous faith and belief in God, waiting was not her strong suit. But Gay's waiting ended today because she received the information she had been impatient for since August 2014, when this conflict began.

Mississippi State Supreme Court made history by swiftly issuing a decision fewer than two days after the hearing on June 13, 2017. The Supreme Judges all agreed that, based on the arguments and evidence presented, all the allegations against Gay should be dismissed. The stress released from an end to her waiting was comparable to a one-hundred-pound weight lifted from Gay's chest. Gay was overwhelmed with gratitude for her victory, and she stood poised to move on.

Gay may never know who wanted to destroy her reputation and career. Three years is a long time of enduring uncertainty; however, she never wavered in her determination to clear her name. Throughout the years of waiting, she remained faithful and possessed no doubts in a victory during the most challenging undertaking of her career. There are a few things that Gay realized about going through this ordeal: first, no matter how successful a person becomes, there is someone who will feel threatened by your accomplishments; second, being grateful and humble for everything in life is important; and third, being a woman with a strong personality can be intimidating for many people, but you must stand up and be true to yourself no matter what happens. Gay continues to do all the things that make her who she is today. This setback did not cause her to change the core of her character. She has proven that in the face of controversy, she possesses the grit, determination, and willingness to stand up for herself.

CHAPTER FOUR

ANGELA STOKES

"LEADER"

February 2016

The guy walked into one of his favorite restaurants. As he entered, he moved swiftly to the counter to place his order, so he was not as attentive as usual. However, someone caught his attention, but he dismissed it because he was focused on the task at hand. He reached the counter and placed his order, while he was waiting, he turned his attention back to the person he had noticed earlier. He looked over and watched as a mature, petite woman with slightly brown hair with a sprinkle of grey along with eyeglasses hiding a troubled look, cleaning tables. As he continued watching, he noticed that although she was cleaning tables, she appeared to be a million miles away in deep thought. Suddenly he realized she looked very familiar and he stared even more at this woman to the point it became noticeable. Finally, he asked if they knew each other. It struck him that he knew exactly who she was. He was in disbelief, but as he got closer to her, indeed he was right and it was her. His mind began racing with many questions because being inquisitive came natural to him. He continued his approach and asked if she was in fact Angela. It was obvious that the woman did not want to talk, and she almost appeared to be frightened by the thought of him knowing who she was that she walked away. Eventually, the woman realized that she was unable to hide so she acknowledged that in fact she was Angela and gave the man her number. It was the man's job to ask questions because he was a reporter who was always looking for a story. The man could not fathom that grabbing a bite to eat at Chick-fil-A in the City of Strongsville would become so eventful. The woman in uniform cleaning tables was Angela Stokes. Yes, Judge Angela Stokes of the well-known and highly respected Stokes political family. The only words that came to mind were "How the mighty have fallen".

The 1960s

Growing up as a young girl during the 1960s was challenging in Cleveland, Ohio. The Civil Rights Movement was beginning to gain momentum, which led to ongoing civil unrest throughout many cities in the United States, including Cleveland. There was one incident during the summer of 1966 which would be life-changing to Angela, her family, and the overall community.

Hough is a neighborhood on the east side of Cleveland. Hough's name derives from Oliver and Elisa Hough, who settled there in 1799. The neighborhood went through many changes over the years, and by 1873 it was well-known for having prominent residents and exclusive schools in Cleveland. But neighborhoods evolve and by the end of World War I, it became home to the white middle class at least up to the mid-1960s, while blacks were only five percent of the residents in Hough. The next transition for Hough came in the mid-1960s when black residents made up eighty-eight percent of the area while white residents left for the suburbs and downtown neighborhoods.

July 18, 1966

There was one incident during the summer of 1966 in one neighborhood in Cleveland which led to changing Angela's life. The property values and economic conditions in Hough gravely changed once blacks were the predominate residents, despite Hough's long history of being a thriving neighborhood. Decreased revenues, higher unemployment, and less city services were just some of the issues facing the black residents in Hough. These factors, along with the sweeping changes of the Civil Rights Movement, manifested in racial unrest in the summer of 1966.

Cleveland was suffering from weeks of a heat wave. Black residents lived in rental buildings, practically on top of each other, with no air conditioning and children had no play areas in which to gather. The hot weather on Monday, July 18, 1966 in Hough could be felt as residents moved slowly throughout the streets, seeking refuge from the scorching sun beating down on their bodies, drenched in their sweat-soaked clothes. The heat wave had already claimed the lives of many, but mostly the elderly. Things had been heating up in Hough, and not just from the heat wave, but the smoldering heat aided in things boiling over into the streets.

Meanwhile, at the Seventy Niner's Café, located at Hough Avenue and East Seventy-Ninth Street, the place was packed with customers, while the jukebox belted out the latest songs such as "You Can't Hurry Love" by The Supremes or "Reach Out I'll Be There" by The Four Tops. The café was owned and operated by Dave and Abe Feigenbaum who were white, just like most of the businesses in the predominately black Hough neighborhood.

It was common back then to ask people to help with funeral expenses. In the early afternoon, a woman entered the café seeking assistance on behalf of the children of her deceased friend. The woman was told no collection would be done and to leave the café. The owners would not help the woman because she was black. Many hours later, a black patron entered the café, asking for a cup of water because it was so hot outside. However, the owners refused his request and told him to leave. A few moments later a sign was posted on the door with the words, "No Water for N____s". Both incidents spread through the neighborhood almost instantly because a crowd of people gathered outside the café. The police arrived quickly at the scene to quiet the crowd; however, the crowd became angrier and began throwing rocks, bottles and bricks.

The police were unable to contain things in Hough as the crowd intensified into an uncontrollable riot. The crowds started burning buildings, vandalizing businesses and residences, and looting was rampant and spread to surrounding neighborhoods. The media and community leaders criticized Mayor Ralph S. Locher's lack of control over the Hough riots and surrounding areas and his failure to address ongoing problems beforehand. After days of rioting and feeling like there were no other options, Mayor Locher requested the National Guard to come to Cleveland to secure and end the riots. The riots ended with four blacks being killed, numerous people injured, several businesses burned or looted, and many blacks arrested.

Angela Stokes was about fourteen years old during the Hough riots. She understood the seriousness of the violence taking place in her community. As much as her family tried to make things normal for a young girl, Angela knew and saw the realities of blacks' struggles for being accepted without threats to their black skin. Although she was frightened by the ongoing riots, she knew that changes were happening. Angela had firsthand knowledge of these truths because she was one of the daughters of the well-known civil rights attorney, Louis Stokes. Louis Stokes had been working for racial equality for the citizens of Cleveland for many years. In fact, Louis Stokes argued the well-known United States Supreme Court case *Terry v. Ohio*, which defined the lawfulness of police search and seizure procedures which is still prevalent today. Also, Angela's uncle was a formidable attorney like his brother, except he decided to directly affect the Cleveland community by entering local politics.

The Hough riots brought realization to the white community about what had been known by blacks for many years of the devastating problems in their neighborhoods. Further, people in Cleveland knew that Mayor Locher was no longer the answer, and they looked to make drastic changes by seeking a candidate who would appeal to both whites and blacks in the community.

Angela's uncle, Carl B. Stokes, stepped up to be the answer to the Cleveland community.

Cleveland, 1967

Carl B. Stokes began his political career by running for Mayor of Cleveland. This campaign was Angela's first experience with politics. Angela, her siblings, and cousins created a group called "Young Folks for Stokes," to aid her uncle's campaign. The group went door to door in different neighborhoods, talking to voters, handing out literature about Carl, and asking for their votes. The group proved to be very effective for the Stokes election. Angela was excited for her active involvement in being a part of history in helping her uncle become mayor. Throughout the campaign, Angela interacted with historical icons like Martin Luther King and Ralph Abernathy, as well as many others who later became known for their roles in history. The campaign was a success because Carl became the first black Mayor of Cleveland, thereby making history, and Angela was there to witness it.

Cleveland, 1969

About two years later, Angela was involved in another historical campaign, when her father chose to enter the political arena and successfully became the first black Congressman from Cleveland. These events left a profound impression on Angela, which carried over into her adulthood. As a young child, Angela deeply respected her father and always followed his advice, which is why she attended college and ultimately law school. Angela was the only sibling who attended law school, like her father and uncle.

Angela was elated to follow in the footsteps of her father and uncle. Angela began her legal career in the corporate area but she shifted jobs and went to work for the government. Angela worked as an Assistant Attorney at the Attorney's General's office in Columbus, Ohio. She'd been working in Columbus for about six years when she received a call from her father telling her it was time to carry on the legacy that he and his brother had built in Cleveland. Angela was unprepared because she was content with her current life but she always obeyed her father. Angela followed her father's wishes by returning to Cleveland to begin the second phase of her life.

Angela's return to Cleveland was just the beginning because her dad and uncle swiftly groomed her for politics. Angela had never imagined herself being in politics, so she was nervous about the process, but she trusted her father's and uncle's judgment. Although she had been exposed to politics as a young girl and enjoyed helping her uncle, it was still a foreign concepti to her. Angela was content being an attorney and working for the government. But Angela's father had bigger plans for her; he wanted Angela to go all the way to Washington, D.C.

But first she had to win a local race. Angela's father was excited that one of his children had decided to follow in his footsteps, and he would be there to help her along the way to see it happen.

Under the political advice of her father and uncle, Angela prepared to campaign for her first judge race. Unfortunately she did not win that election. But her father and uncle were not deterred by the loss. However, Angela felt it was a sign to give up and return to the government. They strongly encouraged Angela to add her name to another upcoming judge seat at Cleveland Municipal Court which was a position that her uncle Carl once filled when she was a little girl. Angela obeyed their advice.

Fall, 1995

In fall 1995, Angela placed her name on the ballot as candidate for judge at Cleveland Municipal Court. Angela was guided by the best political duo in Cleveland. Her father and uncle used their political resources to get Angela elected as judge. Angela followed their advice and did everything she was instructed to do for her campaign. The political duo aided Angela to a victory, and on November 7, 1995, Angela was elected judge for Cleveland Municipal Court. Angela was glad that she had listened to her father's and uncle's advice, and she was ecstatic that she would be the one to carry on the Stokes family name in the political arena.

Cleveland Municipal Court is in the Justice Center downtown. Most people dislike going downtown because the buildings can be perceived as cold and uninviting but especially the Justice Center. Most have preconceived ideas about the court system and how things are done by judges, thereby making it a more stressful undertaking. Most find walking into the Justice Center, which occupies a city block with twenty-five floors, to be a daunting and annoying undertaking, especially when being forced to appear before a judge.

Cleveland Municipal Court primarily handles misdemeanor cases such as traffic violations, vicious dog attacks, prostitution, and other legal matters. Newly elected Municipal Court Judge Stokes began working at the Justice Center in 1996, and she was eager to help the community. Judge Stokes learned from her mentors about being an excellent public servant and she intended to ensure that every person who appeared in her court had access to equal justice and all available resources.

Judge Stokes understood the problems that people had with coming and being in court, but she wanted to do everything within her power to assist them to be better. Judge Stokes's motivation for helping everyone would sometimes result in longer hours than her colleagues', and more insight into each person's situation, with the intent to resolve any ongoing problems.

Judge Stokes, being new at the courthouse, received complaints about her methods, which began circulating throughout the Justice Center. Judge Stokes was very different than her colleagues because most other judges completed their cases early in the afternoon, but Stokes's hours were known to last into the late evening. Additionally, most of her colleagues did not utilize resources such as drug testing. Rather, her colleagues used punishment as the proper way of handling offenders in their courtroom.

Just a few years after Judge Stokes began working at the courthouse, she came to realize the job was challenging because of seeing people at their worse. Nonetheless, she enjoyed helping people who came into court, but wanted to offer better solutions than jail time. In less than three years, Judge Stokes formed a plan which would help people to not be a constant participant in the legal system. She organized a plan that would directly change offenders' lives and make them better and productive citizens for Cleveland.

Judge Stokes organized for the first time a two-day retreat that included all thirteen Cleveland Municipal Court judges gathered to partake in learning about the new program. She created an opportunity for offenders to have a better life than being consumed with drugs and physical abuse. She had figured out a way to prevent some people using the court as a revolving door and help them deal with their problems. Judge Stokes received some positive feedback for offering alternative options to jail. However, she received various complaints from colleagues and some offenders. Many judges perceived the program as causing delays when people would eventually go the jail.

At least one of her colleagues openly expressed displeasure with the program. Judge Ellen Connally publicly complained about Judge Stokes delaying spots because of offenders waiting for the new program. Judge Connally believed that offenders fully knew what they were doing and should be accountable for their actions by serving jail time. However, Judge Stokes believed that all offenders should be offered rehabilitation and a chance to live a better life. Judge Stokes also received sharp disapproval from the offenders. There were several disagreements over pushing religion and praying onto them. Some prostitutes complained about being forced to participate in praying sessions against their will. They saw this as intruding on their rights. The reports over the prayer meetings obtained attention by the Supreme Court of Ohio. After investigating the alleged complaints, they found that Judge Stokes had committed no wrongdoing. These kinds of accusations were just the beginning, because at least one person would be relentless against any progress Judge Stokes attempted to put forth at Cleveland Municipal Court. But it would take years and years of plotting for something to happen.

1998

Judge Stokes founded Project HOPE (Holistic Opportunities and Preventive Education) which offered prostitutes an alternative to going to jail. The program was designed for six to eight weeks of drug rehabilitation, job training, health screening, counseling, and housing for participants. Judge Stokes was proud that she was in a position that allowed her to give back to the community, just like her father taught her when she was a little girl. Judge Stokes wanted to live by the family motto of "serving with excellence and aiming high". Despite Judge Stokes' recent accomplishments, the minor controversy over her methods would unknowingly continue to grow behind the scenes, perpetuated by those who once praised her work methods.

Ronald Adrine was just like Angela; he was also a native of the Cleveland community. He, like many others, were familiar with the Stokes family and their amazing accomplishments throughout Cleveland and beyond. In fact, it is likely one of the reasons Ronald went to law school. Ronald attended Cleveland Marshall College of Law which was the alma mater of the Stokes brothers.

Ronald became an attorney in 1973, after successfully passing the Ohio Bar Exam. Ronald's eyes were wide open to the possibilities of being an attorney. He started out working as a prosecutor for the Cleveland District Attorney's office. After working there for a few years, he chose to work at his father's law office. Ronald kept striving for more, so he wanted to get into politics. There was an open position for a municipal court judge seat, so Ronald decided he would add his name to the ballot.

It was a thrilling time to be running for judge and Ronald wanted to ensure that he would win on his first attempt, so he campaigned by going door to door to ask for voters' support. However, Ronald was determined to be successful, so he approached the Stokes brothers for an endorsement. Ronald knew that having their support would almost guarantee victory on election day. Unfortunately, Ronald had not anticipated that the Stokes brothers would decline to support him. Ronald was surprised by the rejection because he had tremendous respect for the Stokes family. Ronald was more determined to win and continued seeking support for his campaign. Ronald's hard work and tenacity paid off because he won his first election for the judge seat. Although Ronald was successful, there were likely lingering feelings of not being supported by the Stokes brothers, which would be evident in future events of disparagement between Ronald Adrine and Angela Stokes.

Fall 1995

In 1995, Judge Ronald Adrine and Judge Angela Stokes became colleagues. It had been fourteen years since he had become a judge at Cleveland Municipal Court.

Because Judge Stokes was new to the court, typically a more senior judge such as Judge Adrine, would act as a mentor by guiding and offering advice on how to handle cases. Ideally, Judge Adrine would have been the logical mentor for Judge Stokes, since he was very familiar with her family. Yet, Judge Adrine elected to take on a different role regarding Judge Stokes. He was an adversary disguised as a friend. Judge Stokes's initial time at court should have been enjoyable, but instead it became an almost a daily challenge due to initial criticisms, led by constant complaints from her colleagues. As a newcomer, Judge Stokes could not be expected to have the same level of experience as her more senior colleagues, but she was measured at an unreasonable standard.

Taking a position as a judge comes with a learning curve, which is no different than any new job. Still, it was evident that Judge Stokes had enemies based on the frivolous complaints against her. Some people complained that Judge Stokes would not allow whispering in her court room; others complained that she posed to many questions to defendants; that she told people to be quiet in court; and that she used too many resources on her cases. All these criticisms were frivolous and baseless, but they unceasingly cultivated because colleagues wanted her gone from municipal court.

Judge Adrine heard some of the criticisms against Judge Stokes and he acted. Judge Adrine went to Angela's father and gossiped about all her issues at court. When

Judge Stokes discovered what Adrine had done, she was insulted that a colleague would choose to chatter about her instead of approaching her directly with any concerns. It became apparent that Judge Adrine was not her friend.

Their relationship would be one of continuous animosity over the course of their working together. In fact, both Judge Stokes and Judge Adrine constantly filed complaints against each other. Judge Stokes filed a grievance against Judge Adrine for an alleged campaign violation that he used staffers during working hours to send emails about a re-election fundraiser. Judge Adrine regularly filed protests about Judge Stokes's courtroom actions. The bitterness between the two judges continued to surmount over the years and Judge Adrine was determined to have Judge Stokes removed from her courtroom.

Despite the ongoing encounters between Judges Stokes and Adrine, Judge Stokes managed to get re-elected and had been a judge for almost sixteen years. In the 2011 election, at least thirty-five thousand voters overwhelmingly re-elected Judge Stokes to Cleveland Municipal Court. Judge Stokes was delighted to again have successfully won the confidence of the voters. Judge Stokes looked forward to serving the community as she had been doing over last sixteen years.

Judge Stokes's victory was brief because she was destined to face challenges that she never imagined facing since winning her first election in 1995. About two years after her re-election, Judge Stokes became the subject of an investigation over her courtroom demeanor. Apparently, the Ohio Board of Commissioners had been receiving numerous complaints that warranted an examination. The Board assigned a special investigator to review about three hundred complaints against Judge Stokes, dating almost back to when she first became a judge.

After the special investigator reviewed all the grievances against Judge Stokes, he produced a forty-nine-page report outlining the findings of his inquiries. The report highlighted many issues with Judge Stokes's courtroom demeanor, such as her overuse of court resources on tests. Further, the report alluded that a psychiatric evaluation was warranted because some believed her to have a mental illness. Finally, the report recommended that Judge Stokes be removed from court because she allegedly posed a threat as a serious harm to the public as a judge.

The report triggered a local newspaper to publish an editorial calling for Judge Stokes to step down from the bench. However, Judge Stokes refused to remain silent while her character was under attack. Judge Stokes went to *Call and Post* an issue a statement to offer a defense to the editorial. Stokes's statement, in part, said, "I have never had mental health issues and will vigorously defend, in the appropriate forum, any suggestion along these lines."

A few months later, Judge Stokes was under attack by none other than Judge Adrine. Although Judge Stokes had not been formally charged with anything, nor had she been allowed to defend herself againt the pending allegations, Judge Adrine acted against her. Judge Adrine felt he needed to save the public from Judge Stokes. So without any authority, on March 14, 2014, he put forth an order to remove all criminal cases from Judge Stokes. Judge Adrine reassigned all Stokes's criminal cases to other judges but allowed her to continue hearing the civil cases.

Judge Stokes once again stepped up to defend herself from this unsanctioned action by Judge Adrine. Judge Stokes maintained that by removing her criminal cases before she could be heard was a denial of due process, which is violation of constitutional rights. Judge Stokes was rightfully distressed over the ongoing attacks against her without any repercussions to the accusers. Judge Stokes wanted the community to know the truth and had every intention of fighting back to clear her name and reputation.

The final attack against Judge Stokes came on December 18, 2014, when the Ohio Supreme Court suspended her law license before she was afforded an opportunity to defend herself against these allegations. The suspension of Judge Stokes's law license meant she could no longer work as a judge, and she received no income, which forced her into unemployment. Also, a hearing was scheduled in February 2015, which could result in her permanent removal from the bench. A hearing based on demeanor is an unprecedented situation because it is hard to prove. This hearing was a first of its kind in Cleveland, where a judge's character was brought under question at this level of inquiry.

Judge Stokes responded to the latest occurrence by submitting yet another statement expressing her displeasure of how she was being treated. She submitted a 196-page report addressing all allegations, including the suspension of her law license, before being allowed to defend herself. In the report, Judge Stokes cited at least six judges, all of whom were white, who were charged with judicial misconduct, but their law licenses were not suspended, and those judges' actions were comparable, if not worse, than the allegations lodged against Judge Stokes. Furthermore, Judge Stokes stated "It appears that, an African American female, has not been treated in a manner similar to white judges in like circumstances."

Judge Stokes was ready to be heard on February 23, 2015, but it was moved to a few days later because both sides tried to negotiate an agreement, but those conversations were futile. February 26, 2015 was the first day of the hearing against Judge Stokes, which would prove to be a long process because there was a list of 150 witnesses set to testify against her. However, there were two key witnesses who they relied on. Judge Ronald Adrine and Judge Larry Jones both worked at Cleveland

Municipal Court with Judge Stokes. Apparently, their testimonies would be the most disparaging against Judge Stokes, since they worked at court during the time of all the complaints. Judge Adrine testified that Judge Stokes was a problem from the time she started working at municipal court and he viewed her as ongoing problem. It was evident that he disliked Judge Stokes and that his testimony appeared to be more personal than professional. Similarly, Judge Jones gave the same testimony about Judge Stokes, except he did not document anything or encourage people to file complaints.

Judge Stokes had to endure countless testimonies against her while she waited to put on her defense. Judge Stokes expected that her defense would address all the allegations against her with more favorable testimony from at least ninety witnesses. The hearing was held periodically, rather than consistently every day, because of the numerous witnesses on both sides. In between, when the hearing was not taking place, both sides attempted to negotiate a settlement to resolve this matter because it was so time consuming.

Judge Stokes was unprepared for the life changing event that happened on August 18, 2015. Her father, Louis Stokes, passed away. Judge Stokes's father's death was devastating because he was her biggest supporter over the months of the hearings she had to endure. The loss of her father caused Judge Stokes to rethink the hearings and, eventually, a few months after her father's death, she agreed to a settlement.

On December 10, 2015, as part of the settlement, Judge Stokes agreed to officially resign as judge and never seek any judge position in the future, except a federal court appointment. In exchange for Judge Stokes's resignation, all charges against her were dismissed and she would be allowed to regain her law license in the future.

Just a few months after the settlement, Judge Stokes was spotted working at a Chick-fil-A.

The Stokes political legacy ended after being an integral part of the black community because of three hundred unsubstantiated complaints, which averages to about a complaint and a half per month over the sixteen years that Judge Stokes was on the bench. Clearly, this is not a significant number of grievances as was reported, and did not rise to the level of unreasonable scrutiny that Judge Stokes was subjected to over the years.

It is obvious: Judge Stokes was targeted from the moment she won the judge seat until her removal from court. The Stokes name and family connections may have been a great benefit from one perspective, but a downfall due from another. It was never Judge Stokes's intention to get into politics, but she always respected her father's wisdom and advice. Of course, her father could not have foreseen the devastation that would befall his daughter. Likely, the Stokes name carried so much respect for many in the community, which also meant that just as many people disliked the family. Once Judge Stokes got involved, she seemed to have more naysayers than supporters, which is evident from the way she was treated by colleagues and those in authority over her fate.

Louis Stokes wanted his daughter to truly follow in his footsteps by running for Congress after she had been a judge for a few years, but Angela declined because she like being a judge. If either of them could have known what would happen, Judge Stokes would have taken the opportunity to run for Congress over her current situation. However, Judge Stokes once stated that she never really wanted to be involved in anything and that she was content just be an attorney for the government. Well, maybe that was her true calling. As much as Judge Stokes respected her father and wanted to obey him, maybe following her own mind would've been better. This in not to say that she did anything wrong or to give any validity to any of the so-called allegations, but the alternative of being removed as a judge certainly was not the future she envisioned.

CHAPTER FIVE

RHONDA CRAWFORD

"BELIEVER"

April 26, 2018

I t was sunny and mild, as usual that day in Calumet City—which locals call Cal City—as the neighborhood filled up with adults returning home from work and children home from school. Late in the afternoon, this charming neighborhood in Cal City would soon learn how a knock on a door can rapidly change things.

Fall, 1989

Rhonda Crawford is a beautiful person who could light up a room with her positive energy and smile. As a little girl growing up in Englewood on Chicago's south side—a historic neighborhood in the Windy City, dating back to the mid-1800s—Rhonda had many dreams of what she wanted to be when she grew up. Rhonda also knew that education was important, and she knew it would allow her to achieve many goals in life.

During the 1970s and 1980s, Englewood, like many other urban neighborhoods, struggled with white flight, poverty, crime, and declining real estate value, all while the black population increased in the neighborhood. This was the era that Rhonda grew up in: a time when the neighborhood was extremely violent and plagued with limited resources. As a little girl growing up under those conditions, it would have been a challenge for Rhonda to see herself succeeding in life. However, Rhonda was a determined individual, and she would not let anything deter her from her dream of being a nurse.

Rhonda loved growing up in Englewood, and she was a proud student of Lindblom College Preparatory High School. She was a happy graduate of the class of 1989, and was eager to begin her journey into college, then nursing school.

Rhonda enjoyed imagining attending college and making something of herself. She attended college at the

University of Illinois, but later enrolled at Chicago State University because she was accepted into the nursing program. Her hard work paid off in 1996 when she graduated with her nursing degree. She had achieved one of her childhood dreams of helping people by becoming a nurse.

April 26, 2018

The striking of a beating balled fist on the door vibrated throughout the one-story red brick bungalow. The people knocking patiently waited on the steps for someone to open the door. When no one answered, they walked into the home and noticed that it was neat and clean, just like the yard outside.

November, 1996

Rhonda was anxious to get started working as a nurse. Her first job offer came from Christ Hospital and Medical Center's patient care unit. She loved being a nurse because it allowed her to help patients and their families. This job was the reason she wanted to become a nurse as child. Rhonda's bubbly personality, along with her amazing smile, made her a great nurse and her patients loved her. She was kind and gentle, and it showed throughout her work at the hospital.

After almost three years with Christ Hospital and Medical Center, Rhonda wanted to do more and learn a different area of the nursing field while still helping patients.

Rhonda landed a job in the cardiology department at Rush University Medical Center. Rhonda delighted in learning a new area of nursing; however, the hospital had some financial issues, and after only six months, Rhonda had to leave her new position. Rhonda returned to her first love of helping patients, and she began working at Northwestern Memorial Hospital in June 1999. Although she enjoyed returning to work with her patients, there was another childhood dream she wanted to fulfill. In 2000, Rhonda decided to start a new journey by enrolling in college again.

April 26, 2018

The unexpected house guests called out for someone, but only heard sounds of their own voices echoing off the walls. After waiting for someone to respond, they began a short walk to the rooms, because they expected that at least one person should be home.

Fall, 2000

Rhonda began her dream of becoming an attorney by attending law school. She enrolled at Chicago-Kent College of Law. She knew that the next three years would be difficult, but she was up to the challenge, just like when she attended college to become a nurse. She was determined to take on any and all classes that would bring her closer to her second childhood dream.

Rhonda could hardly believe that all her hard work

was about to be realized. She remembered the days of dreaming that she would one day become an attorney. She was grateful that she was able to put herself through law school, and that she survived the grueling three years of classes and countless law school exams. The three years went very quickly, and in Spring 2003 Rhonda graduated. Unfortunately, her celebration was cut short because she had another hurdle to overcome. She had to prepare for, and take, the Illinois State Bar exam in order to become an attorney. Just like in law school, she studied for months so she would pass the exam the first time. Her preparation for the bar exam paid off when she took it in July 2003, and a few months later learned that she had passed. She was ecstatic because her second childhood dream had become a reality. In November 2003, Rhonda could finally call herself Attorney Rhonda Crawford.

April 26, 2018

It seemed like miles to get to the rooms, although it was only a few steps. The bedroom door banged open, like in a scary movie when the monster enters the room. The guests were hoping to find the person they were looking for since they'd arrived a few minutes ago.

August, 2003

The first job Rhonda landed after law school was with the Cook County State Attorney's office, in the criminal appeals division. Just like when she was a nurse, she liked discovering new areas in the legal field.

June, 2004

Rhonda wanted to continue learning more about the legal profession, so she left the Cook County State Attorney's office and went to work at a law office. Although she liked working for the firm, she wanted to be more independent and work in many different areas of law. While Rhonda was in law school, she had the opportunity to work as a law clerk for a summer at the courthouse for Chief Judge Timothy Evans, so when a job opportunity became available, she happily applied and was offered the job.

August, 2011

Rhonda began as a staff attorney for Chief Judge Timothy Evans at municipal court in Chicago. She worked directly for Judge Evans, just like when she was a law student, except this time she was an attorney. After four years at the Daley Center, Rhonda transferred to the municipal courthouse in Markham City, which is just outside of the Chicago area. She essentially was doing the same job as a staff attorney, except that she worked for all of the judges at this location.

July, 2015

Rhonda was always striving for more, and to help those who needed it. She had been an attorney for about thirteen years now, and she decided it was time to take on another challenge. The opportunity arose for a judge seat, and Rhonda made the decision to enter politics. Rhonda added her name to the ballot for the municipal court judge in the upcoming election, even though she was very new to politics. Rhonda was one of three people running for the same judge position. Although she had been an attorney for many years, she was still considered a young attorney in the legal community. Being a politician came with numerous challenges, but as always, Rhonda was able to overcome any and all obstacles on the path to her goals in life.

Once Rhonda became a candidate, she discovered how difficult things can be for a newcomer. One thing that a political candidate must do is raise money to maintain her campaign; however, because Rhonda was new to the legal community, she received little to no financial support. Basically, Rhonda provided most of the money to pay for her own campaign. Rhonda spent approximately thirty-thousand dollars, while the opponents barely spent any of their own money, because they received numerous donations from voters that supported their campaigns.

There are many organizations that make endorsements on who they think voters should support in an election. Several legal groups did not recommend Rhonda, not only because they felt that Rhonda was too young and unknown in the community, but also because she declined to participate in the judge screening process conducted by the organizations. The other two candidates, Anthony Simpkins and Lisa Copland, who were well-known in the community and raised large amounts of money to assist their campaigns, did participate in the judicial screening process, so they were recommended by the legal groups.

However, Rhonda did not allow the lack of support from any organizations, or anyone else, to stop her from campaigning and meeting voters in the community. Rhonda knew that the outcome of any election came from the voters in the community, and she vowed to meet as many people as possible because she was confident that she could win the primary election in March 2016.

March, 2016

Despite the odds against her winning, she continued to campaign against any obstacles placed in her way. She believed in herself and continued to strive for a victory. After Rhonda had been campaigning for months, the primary election on March 15, 2016 finally arrived. The results were astounding because the unknown candidate, Rhonda Crawford, defeated the other candidates by almost forty-seven percent. Now she had to wait a few months for the general election in November before she would be declared a judge.

April 26, 2018

Her eyes were closed, her lips relaxed, her dark skin flawless. She looked peaceful, sleeping in her black t-shirt and black shorts. She did not move when they entered; they assumed she hadn't heard them knocking, or entering the house, because of the earphones playing music, loud enough that they could hear it.

April, 2016

Rhonda knew it was going to be a long eight months, but she was willing to wait. In the meantime, she figured that she would make valuable use of her time by studying judges at her place of work. Because Rhonda was still a staff attorney at Markham courthouse, she had access to all the judges and knew that she could learn a lot by watching them in court. She arrived at work and reviewed the schedule for that day to see what cases were coming before the judges. After looking over the schedule, she determined which cases she wanted to see and went to that judge's courtroom to listen and take notes.

Rhonda wanted to be prepared to take the bench once she was officially declared the winner in November, so it was important for her to learn as much as possible. She had a profound respect for all the municipal court judges and was grateful for the chance to learn from them by "shadowing" their day-to-day activities.

August 11, 2016

It was a typical workday at the Markham Municipal Courthouse. Rhonda arrived early in the morning, like she had every day since she begin working at the courthouse. Rhonda prepared for another day of "shadowing," and decided to sit in on a new judge that she had not watched before, Judge Valarie Turner, who had just transferred to the Markham courthouse. Judge Turner was handling cases for Judge Coughlin this day.

Rhonda entered the court, and Judge Valarie Turner had already begun handling the morning traffic cases, so Rhonda sat nearby, taking notes and observing the judge's techniques. Rhonda was excited to learn from a judge she had not previously shadowed. Judge Turner took a break for lunch and resumed handling the afternoon cases. Rhonda returned to observe the remaining court cases as well.

At one point that afternoon, Judge Turner directed Rhonda to come over to her. Without any notice or discussion with Rhonda, Judge Turner announced to the remaining people in court and court staff, "We're going to switch judges." Judge Turner took off her black robe and motioned for Rhonda to put it on. Rhonda followed the judge's instructions and put on the robe and sat on the judge's bench. Rhonda did not utter any objections to Judge Turner's request and followed her orders.

Rhonda began to handle each case based on step-by-step instructions provided by Judge Turner, who stood next to her throughout the process. The first and second traffic cases were handled swiftly with no objections from anyone. However, the last traffic case pertained to the driver not having proof of valid car insurance. The person stepped up and explained that he did not have his insurance card. The city prosecutor, Luciano Panici, Jr., asked to continue the case and requested a new court date. Judge Turner and Rhonda discussed the case and decided to dismiss the case over the vehement objections by Mr. Panici, Jr. All requests to continue the matter and not dismiss were ignored.

Mr. Panici, Jr.'s face was beet red as his head shook in displeasure with Rhonda's decision. Anyone who observed the exchange knew that Mr. Panici, Jr. strongly disliked the actions taken and he was determined to do something about it. Once court ended, Mr. Panici, Jr. went to his father, Judge Luciano Panici, Sr., and he explained what had happened. After they discussed the events that transpired in court, it was evident that Judge Panici, Sr. was very upset, and he placed a phone call to alert someone of what had transpired in court.

Once Judge Marjorie Laws learned of the disturbing news, she immediately went to the courtroom to confront Judge Turner and Rhonda about what happened. As Judge Laws was walking towards the courtroom, Rhonda appeared. The words of Judge Laws vibrated the walls as she confronted Rhonda and said, "Why would you risk your career for something like this?"

Rhonda answered, "It's the robe, isn't it?"

Judge Laws fired back, "I am reporting you!"

Rhonda said, "He's just mad because I denied his request for a continuance."

Two years is a long time to contemplate thousands of "What-if" scenarios.

The five minutes of wearing the Judge's robe had started a chain reaction of events, each falling one after another, like an avalanche sliding down a mountain. The decision to wear the robe would prove to be an everlasting change for Rhonda. News of Rhonda wearing the judge's robe quickly spread to other judges, attorneys, and court staff at the Markham courthouse. Rapid changes were defining moments in Rhonda's life. Not surprisingly, she was immediately suspended from her job, pending an investigation of what transpired between Judge Turner and her in the courtroom. Rhonda's greatest joy was working in the legal profession. She was elated to learn every day, and help those who needed it. Rhonda was devastated by the decision to suspend her from her job as staff attorney at the courthouse. However, she was hopeful that things would work out and she could return soon.

Rhonda was no quitter, and she vowed to continue her campaign for judge. Since she found herself without a job for the time being, she decided to make use of her free time by meeting voters. She affirmed that she was going to win the upcoming general election in November, and she went out into different neighborhoods, knocking on doors and reminding people to vote for her.

Approximately two weeks after she was suspended from her job, Rhonda was summoned to a meeting at the Markham courthouse to discuss the events of August 11, 2016 and answer questions.

They began to survey the bedroom more closely.

Rhonda had assumed that her dedicated work ethic of over the last five years would yield a favorable decision on getting her job back. However, less than twenty-four hours after her meeting, she received a certified letter stating that she was terminated. Rhonda was disappointed because she truly enjoyed working at the courthouse. Things continued to unravel in Rhonda's life, like a single thread slowly undoing a hem. Next, Rhonda received a letter from the Illinois Disciplinary Commission requesting that she appear to discuss the robe incident.

It had been about a month since the incident, and Rhonda was concerned that the media would depict a one-sided story. Rhonda wanted to make sure that the public knew what really happened with Judge Turner and to assure voters that she was not removing her name from the November ballot. She made the decision to release a statement and hold a press conference on the same day that she was scheduled to attend the meeting with the disciplinary commission. Rhonda was trying to do everything to prove that she was a good person who had simply made one minor mistake in an otherwise flawless career as an attorney.

Rhonda was a strong person who had endured many obstacles, she always pushed her way to be victorious, and she fully expected the same outcome during this meeting with the disciplinary commission. Although she was nervous about the meeting, she remained positive throughout the ordeal. Rhonda and her attorney arrived for the meeting prepared to answer the questions put before her. Rhonda was under a lot of pressure during the meeting. She was hit with numerous questions about herself, her background, education, prior job history, and finally the recent robe incident. However, she wanted to convey that she would be truthful and answered all questions without any hesitation. She wanted to make sure that the panel knew she was very remorseful for her lack of judgment, but she should not be punished severely because her career as an attorney had been unblemished. Rhonda felt as if this one bad incident should not ruin her entire career and life forever.

She hoped to still be allowed to remain a candidate for the November election, and receive a minor reprimand for wearing the robe. She assumed that, because she was upfront and honest from the very beginning, the panel would show some forgiveness for her minor mistake. Rhonda managed to remain calm throughout the meeting, which lasted for hours. After several hours of non-stop questions, the disciplinary meeting finally ended. Unfortunately, Rhonda had to wait for a decision because the panel needed to discuss the situation first.

Rhonda was not the only one subjected to investigation. Judge Turner was also challenged for her part in the robe incident. Judge Turner was reassigned to administrative duties, which meant she would not be allowed to sit on the bench to hear any more cases. Furthermore, Judge Turner had to appear before a similar board as Rhonda, except it was the Judicial Inquiry Board. Once the board completed its investigation, a complaint was filed to have Judge Turner removed permanently from the bench.

They noticed that a gas-powered generator was quietly running, which was very strange because the electricity was not off.

Watching paint dry would have been a pleasant task, compared to waiting two weeks for the panel to decide her fate. Almost two weeks later, Rhonda received the decision from the panel. Her hopes for a positive resolution were dashed when she learned that the disciplinary panel reached a decision against her. The panel decided to seek to suspend Rhonda's law license before the November election would take place. The disciplinary panel just needed the Illinois Supreme Court to agree with their decision, and Rhonda would not become a judge in November.

It was a brisk sixty degrees on Thursday, October 20, 2016 in Cook County. Rhonda was just beginning her day unemployed and waiting on the outcome of her law license being suspended. Rhonda was hoping to continue campaigning by meeting voters because she was still hopeful that things would work out in her favor. Unfortunately, Rhonda's world was collapsing before her, just two months after the short five minutes when she put on a robe. Rhonda learned that she was being criminally indicted on a felony charge of misconduct and a misdemeanor charge of false impersonation of a judge.

In the interim, Judge Turner was still fighting to maintain her job as judge. Judge Turner filed a response to have the recommendation of removal from the bench dismissed. Unfortunately, her request was denied. Judge Turner appeared in a hearing for her removal from the bench before the Illinois Courts Commission. Judge Turner did not get her wish, and it was decided that she would be immediately removed from the bench, based on the diagnosis that Judge Turner was suffering from Alzheimer's. In fact, it's believed that when the robe incident occurred, she was already suffering from Alzheimer's. The committee removed Judge Turner from the bench in December 2017.

They were Calumet City police officers who had been asked to conduct a wellness check on Rhonda Crawford.

Rhonda had gone from realizing a childhood dream of becoming a judge, to being fired, to possibly losing her law license, and now facing criminal charges. The act of putting on Judge Turner's robe turned Rhonda's life into a nightmare. She hoped that this nightmare would end. Instead, the avalanche continued to roll down the mountainside because about nine days before the election, the Illinois Supreme Court agreed with the Illinois Disciplinary Panel's decision and immediately suspended Rhonda's law license. Clearly, the immediate suspension of her law license meant that she would not become a judge in the November election.

A gentle tap on her exposed arm yielded no immediate response. After several attempts to rouse her, it became obvious that something was wrong. Further inspection of the bedroom discovered three mostly empty prescription medication bottles nearby. The cause for concern heightened and they again tried to rouse Rhonda to no avail. All efforts to revive her were futile because it was evident that she was not going to wake up ever again.

On November 9, 2016—election day—Rhonda received the exciting and devastating news all at the same time. The results from the election were overwhelming: she had ninety-nine percent of the votes. But she could not accept the victory because a week earlier her law license had been suspended; therefore, she was disqualified from accepting the judge seat.

The executor for Rhonda received an ominous text message that Rhonda planned to harm herself, and the police should be contacted. During the search of her home, police discovered a handwritten note in the kitchen, titled "Suicide Letter." The note offered details that she had taken the three different medications, along with starting the gas-powered generator. Also, the police began to understand the phrase on her black t-shirt: "Being a person is too complicated. Time to be a unicorn."

The realization that Rhonda's sweet and gentle face, with her Colgate smile, would no longer light up a room was starting to sink in. No more would anyone hear her sweet voice and partake in the kindness she bestowed upon others when she offered to help them. Rhonda, who was first a nurse because she wanted to help those in need, and who later returned to school to become an attorney, ended her life. Although she left a note explaining what she did, she failed to explain why she did it, especially since she was only three days from a criminal trial that was to begin at the Leighton Criminal Courthouse.

Rhonda was a remarkable person with a big heart, whose only goal in life was to help others in need. No one can deny—not even Rhonda herself—that she made a mistake when she put on Judge Turner's robe on that fateful day on August 11, 2016. Rhonda always maintained that she made a mistake and regretted her decision. Rhonda never ran from the truth of the incident at all. She had been practicing law for almost thirteen years without any formal complaints. She sustained her job as staff attorney at the Markham courthouse for almost six years. She was well-liked and known to be proficient and professional in the legal community.

A minor lapse in judgment did not warrant her being fired, losing her law license, being denied accepting the judge seat, and being charged as a criminal. Losing her job meant she had no income, and losing her law license meant she had no means to earn any income. Finally, it was possible that she could go to jail if she was convicted on the pending criminal charges.

Likely, Rhonda felt like she no longer had a place in society because her identity had been shattered in such a short time. Unfortunately, Rhonda decided that she wanted to be back in control of her life, which meant the horrible decision that led to the finality of her life. Rhonda's answer to taking back control of her destiny was by stopping the journey from continuing.

The people of Chicago would never know the positive impact Rhonda would have made in their lives, had she been allowed to accept her victory and become Judge Rhonda Crawford. All the excessive actions taken against Rhonda were clearly based on other motives. It seems that people were threatened by the greatness Rhonda exuded. And it was stated several times over the course of the incident that Rhonda had not apologized in a manner the masses deemed appropriate. But, clearly, destroying this young woman's life and reputation that resulted in a suicide was much better than allowing her to fulfill her lifelong dreams.

CHAPTER 2-DESIRÉE MARY CHARBONNET

1. Troeh, Eve. "This Judge Helps Repeat Defendants Stay Out Of Her Court And The System". The Atlantic, 2020. https://www.theatlantic.com/politics/archive/2016/02/judge-desiree-charbonnet/470490/.

2. Mackel, Travers. "Desiree Charbonnet Resigning As Judge, Expected to Enter mayor's Race". https://www.google.com/amp/s/www.wdsu.com/amp/article/desiree-charbonnet-resigning-as-judge-expected-to-enter-mayors-race/9543260.

3. Rosgaard, Jessica. "Q&A: New Orleans Mayoral Candidate Desiree Charbonnet". https://www.wwno.org/post/qa-new-orleans-mayoral-candidate-desiree-charbonnet.

4. Adelson, Jeff and Williams, Jessica. "Sidney Torres Vs. Desiree Charbonnet Feud Adds New Dimension to New Orleans Mayoral Race". https://www.nola.com/news/article_273168ca-96cc-5c9c-bffb-b2699607cde1.html.

5. "Desiree Charbonnet". http://theneworleanstribune.com/desiree-charbonnet/.

6. Boyd, Kevin. "Why Is Lane Grigsby Attacking Desiree Charbonnet?". https://thehayride.com/2017/10/lane-grigsby-attacking-desiree-charbonnet/.

CHAPTER 3-GAY POLK PAYTON

1. Emily Wagster, 2017. "Court: 'JudgeCutie' Nickname Doesn't Ruffle Judicial Dignity." 2017. AP NEWS. June 16, 2017. https://apnews.com/a5943301d9da4f9285cbe6dd736715ce.

2. "Mississippi Dismisses Ethics Charges Based On Judge Gay Polk-Payton's Use Of Social Media - Political Correctness Gone Too Far." 2017. BarComplaint.Com. November 28, 2017. http://www.barcomplaint.com/issue-with-judges/ mississippi-dismisses-ethics-charges-based-on-judge-gay-polk-paytons-use-of-social-me dia-political-correctness-gone-too-far/.

3. Ballard, Darlene, Rachel Michel, and Meagan Brittain. 2017. "RESPONDENT BRIEF ON BEHALF OF THE MISSISSIPPI COMMISSION ON JUDICIAL PERFORMANCE REPRESENTING THE COMMISSION." https://janeslawblog.files.wordpress.com/2017/06/mjp-brief.pdf.

4. "IN THE SUPREME COURT OF MISSISSIPPI MISSISSIPPI COMMISSION Attorneys for Respondents." https://courts.ms.gov/appellatecourts/ docket/sendPDF.php?f=dc00001_live.SCT.16. JP.1685.80637.1.pdf&c=85532&a=N&s=2.

5. "Forrest County Justice Court Judge, Gay Polk-Payton Is JCJC Black History Guest Speaker."

https://www.leader-call.com/jcjc_news/forrest-county-justice-court-judge-gay-polk-payton-is-jcjc/article_069e516f-354e-5d06-917c-0a189fd54189.html.

6. Staff Reports, 2016. "Signature Q&A: Gay Polk-Payton | Signature Magazine." www.signaturemagazine.ms. April 30, 2016. https://www.signaturemagazine.ms/content/signature-qa-gay-polk-payton.

7. Hattiesburg Patriot. 2017. "1:30pm Livestream of Mississippi Commission on Judicial Performance v. Judge Gay Polk-Payton Tuesday, June 13, 2017." https://hattiesburgpatriot.com/gay-polk-payton-hattiesburg/.

8. gaypolkpayton.com. "Attorney, Songstress, Author, Motivational & Business Speaker." Gay Polk Payton. https://gaypolkpayton.com/gay-up-close.

9. Rodriguez, Katherine. 2017. "State Supreme Court Rules Mississippi Judge Can Call Herself 'JudgeCutie.'" Breitbart. June 18, 2017. https://www.breitbart.com/politics/2017/06/17/state-supreme-court-rules-mississippi-judge-can-call-judgecutie/.

10. Associated Press. 2017. "Court: 'JudgeCutie' Nickname Doesn't Ruffle Judicial Dignity." US News & World Report. U.S. News & World Report. 2017. https://www.usnews.com/news/best-states/mississippi/

articles/2017-06-16/court-judgecutie-nickname-doesnt-ruffle-judicial-dignity.

11. Volokh, Eugene, and Cyan Banister, 2013. "AMICUS CURIAE BRIEF OF THE CENTER FOR COMPETITIVE POLITICS IN SUPPORT OF RESPONDENT, JUDGE GAY POLK-PAYTON" https://www.ifs.org/wp-content/uploads/2013/03/Mi-Commission-on-Judicial-Performance-Amicus.pdf.

12. Diaz, Oliver E, and David Neil McCarty, 2017. "IN THE SUPREME COURT OF MISSISSIPPI MISSISSIPPI COMMISSION Attorneys for Respondents." 2017. https://janeslawblog.files.wordpress.com/2017/06/polk-payton-brief.pdf.

CHAPTER 4-ANGELA STOKES

1. WKYC Staff, 2016 "Court Reinstates Former Judge Angela Stokes' Law License" https://www.wkyc.com/article/news/local/court-reinstates-former-judge-angela-stokes-law-license/95-283470638.

2. Naymik, Mark, 2013. "Cleveland Judge Angela Stokes Draws Well-Deserved Attention of Ohio Supreme Court: Mark Naymik." Cleveland. January 27, 2013. https://www.cleveland.com/naymik/2013/01/cleveland_judge_angela_stokes.html.

3. Naymik, Mark, 2015. "Judge Angela Stokes to Defend Her Courtroom Behavior at Trial after Failing to Reach Last-Minute Settlement." Cleveland. February 24, 2015. https://www.cleveland.com/naymik/2015/02/judge_angela_stokes_to_defend.html.

4. Naymik, Mark, 2014. "Judge Angela Stokes' Law License Should Be Immediately Suspended, Says Ohio Supreme Court's Office of Disciplinary Counsel in New Complaint." Cleveland. November 6, 2014. https://www.cleveland.com/naymik/2014/11/judge_angela_stokes_law_licens.html.

5. Naymik, Mark, 2013. "Cleveland Municipal Court Judge Angela Stokes Says She Will Defend against Court Complaint Recommending She Undergo Psych Exam." Cleveland. October 23, 2013. https://www.cleveland.com/naymik/2013/10/cleveland_

municipal_court_judg_1.html.

6. Rochelle, Angela. n.d. "Angela R. Stokes."
   http://clevelandmunicipalcourt.org/docs/default-source/
   cmc-history/angela-stokes-from-history-of-the-cleveland-
   municipal-court-rev2-18.pdf?sfvrsn=66cc493d_0.

7. Cuyahoga County Community College, "Stokes Initiative-
   Angela Stokes TC
   https://engagedscholarship.csuohio.edu/cgi/viewcontent.

8. Cleveland 19 Digital Team, 2015. "Testimony Begins in
   Hearing on Judge Angela Stokes Courtroom Behavior."
   https://www.Cleveland19.Com.
   https://www.cleveland19.com/story/28211798/testimony-
   begins-in-hearing-on-judge-angela-stokes-courtroom-
   behavior.

9. Praise Cleveland Staff, 2015. "Judge Angela Stokes Signs
   Off On Deal To Retire." 2015. Praise Cleveland. December
   23, 2015.
   https://praisecleveland.com/1991194/local-news-judge-
   angela-stokes-signs-off-on-deal-to-retire/.

10. Pelzer, Jeremy, 2015. "Complaints about Judge Angela
    Stokes Started Soon after She Took the Bench, Presiding
    Cleveland Judge Testifies." Cleveland. April 9, 2015.
    https://www.cleveland.com/open/index.ssf/2015/04/judge_
    angela_stokes.html.

11. Pelzer, Jeremy, 2015. "Presiding Cleveland Judge Grilled

about Complaints against Judge Angela Stokes." Cleveland.
April 11, 2015.
http://www.cleveland.com/open/index.ssf/2015/04/
presiding_cleveland_judge_gril.html.

12. Grzegorek, Vince, 2015. "Former Judge Angela Stokes Got
Her Law License Back." Cleveland Scene. April 10, 2015.
https://www.clevescene.com/scene-and-heard/
archives/2016/07/28/former-judge-angela-stokes-got-her-
law-license-back.

13. C. Ellen Connally, 2015. "The Resignation of Angela
Stokes: The End of a Political Dynasty." Coolcleveland.
Com. December 2015.
https://coolcleveland.com/2015/12/the-resignation-of-
angela-stokes-the-end-of-a-political-dynasty-by-c-ellen-
connally/.

14. Kevin Niedermier, 2015. "Disciplinary Board Will Decide
the Future for Cleveland Judge Angela Stokes." WKSU.
February 23, 2015.
http://www.wksu.org/news/story/42025.

15. Naymik, Mark. 2015. "Judge Angela Stokes' Trial
Takeaways from Day Two." Cleveland. February 28, 2015.
https://www.cleveland.com/naymik/index.ssf/2015/02/
judge_angela_stokes_trial_take.html#incart_related_
stories.

16. "Robe Probe - Judge ANGELA STOKES, JUDGE." n.d.
www.robeprobe.com.

http://www.robeprobe.com/vote_judge.php?judge_
id=2536&judge_Angela_R._Stokes.

17. Doug Brown, 2013. "An Asshole With a Gavel: Read the
Document Detailing Abuse By Cleveland Judge Angela
Stokes." Cleveland Scene. October 18, 2013.
https://m.clevescene.com/scene-and-heard/
archives/2013/10/18/an-asshole-with-a-gavel-read-the-
document-detailing-abuse-by-cleveland-judge-angela-
stokes.

18. "Angela R. Stokes." Ballotpedia.
https://ballotpedia.org/Angela_R._Stokes.

19. Mark Urycki, 2016. "The Spark That Set Hough on Fire in
July 1966." Ideastream. July 12, 2016.
https://www.ideastream.org/news/the-spark-that-set-
hough-on-fire-in-july-1966.

20. Lapeyrolerie, Olivia. 2015. "EngagedScholarship@
CSU 'No Water for Niggers': The Hough Riots and the
Historiography of the Civil Rights Movement."
https://engagedscholarship.csuohio.edu/cgi/viewcontent.
cgi?article=1027&context=clevmembks.

21. Murray, Kyla. 2017. "Cleveland's Hough Riots of 1966."
December 5, 2017.
https://www.blackpast.org/african-american-history/
cleveland-s-hough-riots-of-1966/.

22. "HOUGH RIOTS." 2018. Encyclopedia of Cleveland

History | Case Western Reserve University. May 11, 2018. https://case.edu/ech/articles/h/hough-riots.

23. "Little Known Black History Fact: Hough Riots." 2018. Black America Web. July 19, 2018. https://blackamericaweb.com/2018/07/19/little-known-black-history-fact-hough-riots/.

CHAPTER 5-RHONDA CRAWFORD

1. LeBien, Mark, and Chicago Tribune. "Rhonda Crawford Statement." https://www.documentcloud.org/documents/3112165-Rhonda-Crawford-Statement.html.

2. In re: Rhonda Crawford [2016] (SUPREME COURT OF ILLINOIS). https://courts.illinois.gov/supremecourt/SpecialMatters/2016/101316_28341_AIS.pdf

3. In re: Rhonda Crawford [2016] (ILLINOIS ATTORNEY REGISTRATION AND DISCIPLINARY COMMISSION). http://dig.abclocal.go.com/wls/documents/2016/Deposition-9-22-16.pdf

4. Rhonda Crawford - Ballotpedia. https://ballotpedia.org/Rhonda_Crawford

5. Ebron, S., 2016. Judge Rhonda Crawford Conceived And Believed But May Fail To Achieve - Courtroom5. https://courtroom5.com/judge-rhonda-crawford-conceived-believed-may-fail-to-achieve

6. Tribune), M., 2016. Illinois ARDC Complaint Vs. Rhonda Crawford. http://www.documentcloud.org/documents/3142113-Illinois-ARDC-Complaint-vs-Rhonda-Crawford.html

7. Luperon, A., 2018. On Trial For Allegedly Impersonating Judge, Lawyer Dies In Suspected Suicide. https://lawandcrime.com/high-profile/on-trial-for-allegedly-impersonating-judge-lawyer-dies-in-suspected-suicide

8. Lighty, T., 2018. Records Detail Orderly Suicide Of Lawyer Accused Of Impersonating Cook County Judge https://www.chicagotribune.com/news/local/breaking/ct-met-fake-judge-rhonda-crawford-suicide-20180717-story.html

9. 2016. In The Matter Of: RHONDA CRAWFORD. Jerome Larkin. https://www.americanbar.org/content/dam/aba/publications/litigation_news/crawford-complaint.pdf

10. Chicago Staff, 2016. 1st Subcircuit — Hopkins Vacancy. Chicago Daily Law Bulletin. http://www.chicagolawbulletin.com/archives/2016/03/09/hopkins-vacancy-3-9-16.aspx

11. Underhill, K., 2016. Lawyer Indicted For Impersonating A Judge Is Elected To Be Real Judge. Lowering the Bar. https://loweringthebar.net/2016/11/lawyer-indicted-wins.html

12. Board, The Editorial., 2016. Keep The Fake Judge Off The Bench. chicagotribune.com. https://www.chicagotribune.com/opinion/editorials/ct-rhonda-crawford-judge-evans-edit-1017-jm-20161014-story.html

13. Tarm, M., 2016. States Grapple With How To Pick Judges; No Universal System. The Washington Times. https://m.washingtontimes.com/news/2016/nov/5/states-grapple-with-how-to-pick-judges-no-universal

About the Author

Taetrece Harrison happily lives in New Orleans, Louisiana, she fights for justice by day as an attorney and by night she puts on her author or poetry hat depending on her mood.

When she is not in court, you can always find her enjoying the numerous festivals in the city, experiencing a Mardi Gras parade and passionately supporting the New Orleans Saints football team!!!

Taetrece is publishing her first book, which is filled with women's stories her first book titled "Bitch Hunt" she felt "needed to be told".

Printed in Great Britain
by Amazon